Whispers of God
TO A
Hungry Heart

Growing in God's Love 'memoir' for the Devotional Reader

GLENDA VINSON
KENNEMORE

WESTBOW
PRESS®
A DIVISION OF THOMAS NELSON
& ZONDERVAN

WestBow Press books may be ordered through booksellers or by contacting:

WestBow Press
A Division of Thomas Nelson & Zondervan
1663 Liberty Drive
Bloomington, IN 47403
www.westbowpress.com
844-714-3454

ISBN: 978-1-6642-0822-3 (sc)
ISBN: 978-1-6642-0824-7 (hc)
ISBN: 978-1-6642-0823-0 (e)

Library of Congress Control Number: 2020919447

Print information available on the last page.

WestBow Press rev. date: 11/19/2020

Especially for

_____

From

_____

Date _____

Encounter God's heart and hear his gentle voice. God delights in hearing from us. He listens to our songs and sighs, and he answers us with words of love and truth. This daily *devotional* contains '*Whispers of God to the Hungry Heart*' of his people. Each insight I hope will encourage you with his words of comfort, joy, and unconditional love. Lean into God's presence and enjoy his peace today and every day. God's timing. There is no force so powerful as an idea whose time has come. God will prepare us for our 'special moment'.

To Heidi, Brittany and Jarrode I hope you find within yourself the kind of happiness that withstands the ups and downs of life. No one should have the power to limit or repress your happiness. For you are well LOVED.

To my husband Patrick thank you for always encouraging my heart and having the faith of uplifting me when I needed it the most.

"NO MAN IS GREATER THAN HIS PRAYER LIFE"

CONTENTS

INTRODUCTION

Tracing the pathways of my 'dedication' story leads me to discover some significant pathways that have played a big part in my life. In particular, my *'journey'* with simple faith inspired me to follow Christ. Moments in our life is living within us it is considered as a 'good story'. At times it is visible, tangible, ready to be lived that it must be told. This is the feeling that led me in search 'within' to write **'Whispers of God to a Hungry Heart.'** Let not our dreams disappear and considered as a 'disappointment'. I want the next 20 years to count for something—to mean something to someone, to make an impact, to tell of my story with a creative positive way. Parts of my stories are not perfect, but it is mine. I want to liberate people from their fears give 'insight to mine' to let them know there is a 'God' and that they 'belong' and are capable of living out their dreams too... We all need to start pursuing a life filled with beauty, and depth in a *'purposeful pathway'*. The golden link is well-known and has massive potential to be done anywhere, at anytime. This could be the beginning of someone else's epic story and one more moment of realizing mine.

LET GOD GIVE IT!

SPECIAL WORDS

- Sell all you have and Give to the Poor
- Why Jesus folded the burial cloth after His resurrection
- Red like Crimson
- Decide what is Right or Wrong
- Walking in the Realm
- Does God Answer *'Whispering Prayers'* when we are in 'Doubt'?
- 'No Chance or Luck for the Godly'
- God's Perfect Time
- Jesus Crushed Satan
- Tithing
- Definitions of Prosperity
- The Divine Exchange covers *'salvation'*
- Move Forward - Double for your Trouble

God's Notes

Whispers of God to a *Hungry Heart*
growing in God's love 'memoir' for the devotional reader
www.facebook.com/@creationofhope/Inspirational Words

No matter how we feel,
God knows and understands—
He lifts us and sets us upon a Rock
And takes us by the hand...
Lead me to that Rock that is higher
Than I...

The emptiness inside of me,
Lay quiet, cold and still;
Awash with hollow hunger,
Longing to be filled...

big things
small beginnings...

'AWAKENING'

In 1994, my daughter had just died, and I was searching. I began to keep a daily journal, pray, and read Bible verses — all completely new to me I had grown up in a Christian atmosphere as a child but did not know the true God in fullness. I felt a deep awakening in my heart, and power was flowing into me as I lit candles to proceed to whisper prayers to God daily in my thoughts. Through prayer and Bible reading, I began to understand for the first time how empty my heart felt. I had a hunger to be filled. I was at home going through each room trying to feel my daughter's presence. Tears ran down my cheeks. As I picked up the Bible, I started searching I was wanting and learning for myself finding out some things I was brought up as a child was not what I was learning from the Bible. Through research, I start to read my Bible more.

From reading, I finally realized I was hearing the 'whispers of God'. God was accomplishing His purposes in me and whispering His love through powerful means: reading His Word about His people. God had begun a good work in me.

Today, I treasure those memories as major milestones on my faith journey. Long before I knew God, He knew me and loved me. He placed His Word in my life at a time of 'hunger and sadness' and opened my eyes to see I had all the books I needed to do research to sow seeds of faith into my life — seeds that have grown into a vibrant personal friendship with God which continue to grow ever-deeper roots.

PRAYER

Dear Lord, thank You for beginning Your good work in our lives and using Your Word and Your people to complete it. Stir our hunger for Your Word. Thank You for Your love in our lives. Thank You for setting the table with Your mercy and grace. In Jesus's name, amen.

Long before I knew God, He knew me and loved me. During a death, a curtain was pulled back to peer deep into my soul, where my hunger originated. I knew I was reading truth. This is God, who inspired me to search for Him.

I am not a fiction reader. I always want to read something that is concrete and can sink down within me. God knew this. He said, "Glenda, pick up that Life Application Bible. You have dictionaries the Bible a Merriam-Webster dictionary, a who's who book, etc." This is how God whispers to you.

'SALVATION'

When I was young in the late 1970s and early 1980s, I watched Christian shows on TV and saw people such as; Rex Humbard, Oral Roberts, and Robert Schuller.

The quote I loved from Robert Schuller was "Anyone can count the seeds in an apple, but only God can count the number of apples in a seed." I didn't realize this quote until 2019 when I had a seed and planted it and then I saw three sprouts come out of it. When I was watching Rex Humbard I was so inspired I realized I had never 'whispered' the prayer of accepting Christ into my heart. I believe I was about eighteen to nineteen years old. After watching one of his shows, I stood up and went into my closet to pray. I whispered *the words* "Lord come into my heart." After whispering this prayer, I started telling God everything that was going on with my life and that I needed Him. Tears came trickling down my cheeks I was a crushed spirit and didn't realize it. I was looking for hope. I was on my knees, and when I stood up and came out of my closet, I peeped out my window. The *flowers* and the *sky* were more vibrant and I felt a safety, peace, of serenity come over my being. I knew right then God had come visited me in the middle of the day and showed me His presence and peace.

Oral Roberts knowledgeably taught the expectation of God's wonderful mercy and grace so that we may remain constantly victorious in our faith. He always stated "Something good is going to happen to you."

Thank God for the inspirational shows that had drew my interest into salvation.

Hear me, LORD, and answer me,
for I am poor and needy.
Guard my life, for I am faithful to you;
save your servant who trusts in you.
Psalm 86:2-3 (NIV).

'WAITING'

One time in the year of 1984, I was struggling. I did a lot of soul searching. I was about twenty eight years old with a small daughter about three years old. I was trying to fill my life with meaning.

I started night school. I studied hard. I felt God's presence, and I knew His peace. One evening the teacher stated "I am going to give a test and anyone who does not pass this test 'will not advance'." I said "Oh, my God, I need Your help!" I studied hard every afternoon. The evening drew nigh when it was time for the test, and I was ready. I was eager for the test, not knowing what the outcome was going to be. I whispered to God, and God knew how important this was to me. I had taken the test and then had to wait another week for the outcome. I started whispering a prayer "Lord I have done my part. Now I need You to do the other part for me." The results were to come back the following week. There were about fifteen to twenty people in the class. Everyone was waiting for the results. The teacher stood in front and stated, "I hate to tell my class that only one person passed the test." My heart dropped so low. I was devastated and sad. Then she proceeded to say, "I am going to tell you the name of the person who passed and I am telling everyone in here you will have to take this class over and retake your test once again to advance yourself." I said, "God I don't have the time to retest" The teacher gave a smile and said, "The name is 'Glenda'" Oh,

That was me! "She is the only one who passed this test." Chills came fluttering all over my body. I could not believe it was my name she called. I passed. God knew my heart.... *What a loving Savior!*

PRAYER

Come, oh blessed Savior, and nourish my soul with heavenly food. Father, thank You for providing us with the helmet of salvation, the hope of Your ultimate justice and ultimate peace a hope that will be realized. We know that things are not nearly as bad as they could be, or even as bad as they will be. But we thank You for the constant assurance. In Christ Jesus amen.

'THIRSTY'

I moved from Curtice, Ohio to Temperance, Michigan bordering Toledo, Ohio. I had now passed my test and now what would I do? I enrolled in an accounting class and a typing class. I thought, This will be interesting. We only had one vehicle I had to rely on this vehicle, and I needed it on Tuesdays and Thursdays so I could have transportation. The night school was one mile down Dean Road. I couldn't miss any accounting classes because the teacher gave work at each session to complete before the next time. One night I didn't have the vehicle, so I had to get a babysitter and walk to school. At night it was spooky. The air was fresh, but I knew in my heart I had to do this as I walked and prayed on my way home. I breathed in the air and fixed my mind on fitness as I walked. I had to do this a few times. I completed all my classes. I was studying the Bible in the afternoon. It had been a long time since I opened the Bible. *I was thirsty for meaning to my life.* In the midst of my soul searching I started to read the Bible every time I could find quietness. I was questioning a lot as I was reading.

"We don't simply endure our hardships, but we can delight in them because they are telling a story far greater than could otherwise be told."

Mercy unto you, and peace, and love, be multiplied.
Jude 2:2 (KJV).

As I was studying, I came across where God said, "Feed my lambs" in John 21:15, 25 (NIV): "Feed my lambs, Feed my sheep." I said, "Lord what is the difference between the lambs and the sheep?" "I whispered to God about What am I reading?" I decided I was going to find a church where I could learn more. I found a church in downtown Temperance no more than a mile or so from my house. It was a Lutheran/Methodist church that had been converted into a born again Christian charismatic church. I decided to get myself together and go to this church. I arrived, and there were many people I sat in the second-to-last pew to listen to the minister. As he was talking, he stopped and said, "Let me tell you about the difference between lambs and sheep I said Humm. I want to hear this. "He gave his explanation, and I soaked it up. The key difference between lambs and sheep is that the word sheep refers to the adult animal while lambs refers to baby sheep in their first year. I whispered to God Thank You, Lord."

The Father said He knows us before we are formed in our mothers' wombs. I find confidence in this. He has been with me all along my faith journey. As we face this day, remember we are not alone. God goes before us to prepare the future. He walks with us in the present.

For you created my inmost being;
you knit me together in my mother's womb. I praise
you because I am fearfully and wonderfully made; your
works are wonderful, I know that full well.
Psalm 139:13-14 (NIV).

IN CHRIST'S STRENGTH

Father I am so Thankful for the Strength that is mine as a Christian. I can not do anything on my own, but through Christ, I can do all things. It is comforting to know that the word all includes the circumstances and concerns in our life that we bring to You this day. I lay them at Your feet, Lord. I take You at your Word knowing you know what is best for me. I can do all things through Jesus who lives in me and loves me. amen.

...I am accustomed to any and every situation—to being filled and being hungry, to having plenty and having need.

I can do all this through him who gives me strength. Philippians 4:13 (NIV).

'EARNEST'

One time when I was only about 10yrs old I walked out of church to get peace within myself. The church was so loud and I needed to find an assurance and quietness. It was in the evening and the sky had many stars it was calm with no breeze. I bowed down on my knees and placed my hands together and I whispered, *"God are you really there?"* As soon as I spoke those words from my mouth someone came walking towards me while I was on my knees. I jumped up quickly being embarrassed I knew they didn't know what I was doing. I yearned to feel God's presence in my life. The person swiftly walks away.

Feeling God's presence there is no age preferential difference where God talks to us. Look at the story Samuel.

I Samuel 3:4-10 (ERV).
The Lord called Samuel, and Samuel answered, "Here I am." Samuel thought Eli was calling him, so he ran to Eli and said, "Here I am. You called me."

But Eli said, "I didn't call you. Go back to bed."

So Samuel went back to bed. Again the Lord called, "Samuel!" Again Samuel ran to Eli and said, "Here I am. You called me."

Eli said, "I didn't call you. Go back to bed." Samuel did not yet know the Lord because the Lord had not spoken directly to him before. The Lord called Samuel the third time. Again Samuel got up and went to Eli and said, "Here I am. You called me." Finally, Eli understood that the Lord was calling the boy. Eli told Samuel, "Go to bed. If he calls you again, say, 'Speak, Lord. I am your servant, and I am listening.'"

So Samuel went back to bed. The Lord came and stood there. He called as he did before, saying, "Samuel, Samuel!"

Samuel said, "Speak. I am your servant, and I am listening."

For I told him that I would judge his family forever because of the sin he knew about; his sons blasphemed God, and he failed to restrain them. I Samuel 3:13 (NIV).

God told Samuel He would punish Eli's family forever because Eli's sons were saying and doing bad things against God. Eli failed to control his sons.

Eli was worthless as a priest, and a failure as a father. He let the grossest kind of evil abide in his own household. But he himself seems to have been a believer. He was slow to hear, but he knew the voice of the Lord when he heard it, and he did not resist or try to defend himself when God pronounced judgment on his household.

Hezekiah states in Isaiah 38:19 (NIV). The living, the living they praise you, as I am doing today; parents tell their children about your faithfulness.

These words should show each of us we need to tell our children about God's Amazing Grace.

'FILLED WITH LOVE'

L ord, let my home be a comforting haven for my family and friends. Let it be a place where they can momentarily escape the pressures of life. Guard our home as well, God, that no harm will fall on it as we are away. May it continue to be a sanctuary of blessing, comfort, and love for each one of us. Let it always be a restful place for our tired bodies at the end of the day. Continue to protect us. Help me do my best to make it a place where people will know they are loved by me and more importantly, by You. amen!

I recall the song **WHISPER A PRAYER**

Whisper a prayer in the morning,
Whisper a prayer at noon,
Whisper a prayer in the evening,
To keep your heart in tune.

God answers prayer in the morning,
God answers prayer at noon.
God answers prayer in the evening,
So keep your heart in tune...

...the idea of whispering a prayer suggests the idea of private prayer where one shuts his door and prays to the Father in secret: See Matt. 6:5 (NIV).

The Lord your God is in your midst, a mighty one who will save; he will rejoice over you with gladness; he will quiet you by his love; he will exult over you with loud singing. Zephaniah 3:17 (ESV).

He will quiet us with his love. That really spoke to me. His love takes delight in us, and that settles us, offering a sense of peace. The underlying message for me was that God loves us just as we are.

God's Grace provides the motivation, through the Holy Spirit the Power through small whisperings to get His work done on earth.

The truth is that God is always whispering to us, we just aren't listening.

We are often hard hearing. And God doesn't like to shout. In fact, God most often whispers to us softly and quietly.

This verse demonstrates that.

"Your own ears will hear him. Right behind you a voice will say, 'This is the way you should go,' whether to the right or to the left." Isaiah 30:21 (NLT).

Our ear will hear a voice behind us, like someone whispering over our shoulder into our ear, Go right or go left or Keep going forward.

'SMALL STILL VOICE'

When Elijah ran from the threats of Jezebel and hid in a cave on Mount Horeb, I Kings 19:9 (NIV) he heard from the voice of God. Elijah heard from God frequently (he was a prophet after all), but God wanted to make sure Elijah heard Him. So God whispered. A strong wind, earthquake and fire all passed by Elijah, but God was not in any of them. God was in a still, small voice.

God was in the whisper

God doesn't like to shout. He loves to guide us gently and purposefully as our loving, heavenly Father. He longs to whisper into our ear, "This is the way, walk in it".

In order to hear God whisper, we have to get close to Him.

Hearing God whisper requires spending time alone with Him, daily and throughout every day. We won't hear Him if we aren't near Him. Don't rush headlong into our day without time alone with God.

'PRAISERS'

W hen I wake up I start to pray. I lay and hug my pillow in the mornings and start telling God about the people who needs His blessings. I praise him for the many things that are answered and what is needed. This is exactly what Jehoshaphat did in battle. He sent out the praisers first.

Just as Jehoshaphat sent the singers and musicians out at the head of the army, and also worshiped God after the battle.

We've probably been there at some point in our life, with a mountain that looked insurmountable. In the case of Israel though, defeat meant at least captivity by their foes and probably death. Greatly outnumbered, the army of Israel appeared to be doomed. In the natural, things looked bad, but all things are possible with God.

Read II Chronicles 20:15–17 (KJV).

The night before the battle, 'God's Spirit' came upon the Levite Jahaziel with a great word. ...Be not afraid nor dismayed by reason of this great multitude; for the battle is not yours, but God's...

This is exactly the kind of word we want from the Lord when facing the impossible, isn't it? The passage says that Jehoshaphat and all of Israel worshiped the Lord, some probably kneeling, some bowing, and some lying prostrate before Him. We also see here that being led by the Levites, some stood and praised God with a loud voice!

'HE'S IN CONTROL'

Thank You, Lord, that the plan You have for our life is Jesus Christ. Without Jesus we wouldn't have eternal life. Thank You Lord for letting us understand, but You know what's best, and everything that happens is for a reason—that You might be glorified. We are so glad that You are in control.

In Jesus's name amen.

Many are the plans in a person's heart, but it is the LORD's purpose that prevails. Proverbs 19:21 (NIV).

A word was secretly brought to me, my ears caught a *whisper* of it. Job 4:12 (NIV).

The words of a whisperer are like delicious morsels; they go down into the inner parts of the body. Proverbs 18:8 (ESV).

'EAGER'

When I first came on facebook I was eager to do something more. I had a lot of notes stored up and wanted to utilize my notes. A whisper came forth into my heart of people in need of God's encouragement. I receive a few people through referral through messenger attending to my thoughts and notes of God. After awhile I had about twenty people. I was doing a ministry on the side. One day a whisper came forth to create a post for the Lord with a picture with words. I was encouraged and created a page called Inspirational Words. I daily post words with pictures honoring God. I started with one soul and it grew to many beautiful souls. Inspirational Words is active and flowing by the Grace of God. Do not ignore the whispers or instincts that come forth in our life as being a Christian. God may be whispering to our heart and we must listen and do something about it. He will make us succeed even our efforts. When we have the Lord with us then we will prosper - "In everything you do, put God first, and He will direct you and crown your *efforts* with success...Proverbs 3:6 (KJV). God had taken my old ability freelance work to utilize for him.

since what may be known about God is plain to them, because God has made it plain to them. Romans 1:19 (NIV).

'TRUST IN HIS GUIDANCE'

Father, today we come before You and we Praise You. You are good and loving. You have our best interests at heart. Take our hand and lead us. Show us the way we should go. In Christ Jesus amen.

Let the morning bring me word of your unfailing love, for I have put my trust in you. Show me the way I should go, for to you I entrust my life. Psalm 143:8 (NIV).

…"The prayer of a righteous person is powerful and effective". James 5:16 (NIV).

'EQUAL FOOTING'

One time I was downtown in the parking lot of the Hartsfield Jackson Atlanta International Airport. Patrick started to park in the back far away from our destination. I said to him, whisper a prayer to God for a parking place. Right after Patrick whispered the prayer we gained a parking place right up front right next to the staircase where we are to enter. Did God tell me to tell him to whisper that prayer? I believe so. God is no respecter of persons. The Bible tells us that God the Father is no respecter of persons. There are also several other verses from Scripture that tell us that God will be showing no partiality or favoritism towards any man or any woman that He has ever created. What this means is that we are all on an equal footing with the Lord and we all have an equal standing with Him.

I Pray that the Lord
Will touch your life today
And that you'll feel His presence
In a new and special way...

'HOUR OF NEED'

The *whispers* of God come to us in our hour of need especially when we are hurting, discouraged, needing direction or disappointed just like Elijah. He was hidden away in a cave, but God knew where to find him. And God knows where to find us as well. Sometimes the Lord speaks early in the morning, in the afternoon, or late at night and even in our dreams to our hearts.

You have searched me, LORD, and you know me. You know when I sit and when I rise; you perceive my thoughts from afar. You discern my going out and my lying down; you are familiar with all my ways. Before a word is on my tongue you, LORD, know it completely. Psalm 139:1- 4 (NIV).

The Bible reminds us over and over again of the comfort and peace that comes from being known and loved by God. We are truly known and perfectly loved, even more clearly and truly than we know and love ourselves!

Since God knows us better than we even know ourselves, we are free to take a deep breath, open our hands, and with humble hearts say to God, Even in the midst of chaos and great pain, I trust that you know my deepest need.

PRAYER

Father God, thank You for loving me. Thank You for choosing me and empowering me to become all that You called me to be. Today, I choose to set my heart and mind on You, I choose to declare Your Word and follow Your ways so that I may walk with You. In Jesus's name I pray. amen.

'YES'

I think about Kathryn Kuhlman when she said God's first choice for her assignment she knew that a man was initially chosen for that role, but because he said No to the Holy Spirit, it then came to her and she said Yes.

It kinda makes me feel like I had said Yes Lord here I am needing your Touch. When God sees a hungry heart He is going to do something with that person. We got to be ready for that moment. God will come and intercede when we call upon Him to place oneself before the throne of God and to stand in the gap for others as well as our self.

'A GODLY EXAMPLE'

God, help me to be an example of a faithful disciple of Christ to my family and friends. I pray that all I do and say will honor You and that I will never be a stumbling block to others. May all within my sphere of influence find me faithful to You. In Christ Jesus amen.

The righteous choose their friends carefully, but the way of the wicked leads them astray. Proverbs 12:26 (NIV).

'HEALING'

This is a true story about *whispering a* prayer to God about some ducks. This story is about my husband and some ducks. The traffic was really bad and a momma duck and her babies were crossing the road and no-one would stop and help them. My husband circled around and went back to them someone ran over the momma and four of her babies and she was trying to make it across the street. The four babies were dead. Patrick parked to the side and went out to the street and picked up the momma duck and laid her in the shade and he laid his hand on her and he said a prayer, Father, I know you care about people and I know you care for this momma duck and her babies who depend upon her so, I ask in the name of the Father for her to be healed.

As soon as he was finished whispering this prayer she flopped out of his hands and wobbled down to her remaining fourteen babies. She went down the ditch towards the water as if nothing had taken place. God healed the momma duck instantly.

Prayer for Healing
By the light and truth of Jesus
I lift my loved one to you.
By the hope of the Redeemer,
I pray for your healing power to break through…

'HONORING'

ᛁ**O**ᛁ

We drove to Cherokee, NC to get away from the house and we stopped at this restaurant hoping to have a good buffet, as we sat down Patrick takes his hat off. As I sat down with my plate he begins to whisper a prayer. I folded my hands and allow him to say the blessing over our food. When we were done this gentleman who I think was around seventy years old came over and said, "I watched you pray I have something I want to give you" (so he excused himself). He went out to his vehicle. He came back with a CD that he had created with another gentleman of Christian music. He said, "I felt to give this CD to you." I looked at him, "I said you are a blessing you have just blessed us" he said. "I am the one who is blessed." I looked back at him, "I said God is Good" and he said, "You have just put chills down my arm." I stood up and hugged him for his kindness and Patrick was just totally beside himself thinking of this man. The man said, "I live in Maggie Valley, down the road and watching you pray you have blessed me." Patrick and I looked at each other after he left and we both had tears in our eyes. Patrick said, "You, know when you honor God – God Honors You." He continued to talk and said, "We have been honored this evening by God." Our God is wonderful,

He inspires the hearts of others a man a total stranger who was kind to us.

...Whether, then, you eat or drink or whatever you do, do all to the glory of God.... I Corinthians 10:31 (NIV).

'BE DELIGHTED WITH THE LORD'

Oh God, thank You so much for the privilege of communing with You. You are so awesome that I cannot express my profound adoration. I delight in you Lord, your law is written within me. Thank You, Lord for coming into my life and transforming my *heart*. In Christ Jesus, amen.

May the glory of the LORD endure forever; may the LORD rejoice in his works— Psalm 104:31 (NIV).

So it is right that I should feel as I do about all of you, for you have a *special* place in my heart. You share with me the special favor of God…
Philippians 1:7 (NLT).

'TRUST AND OBEY'

God wants us to feel useful and needed and fulfilled. To contribute to the world around us in meaningful ways. The ways that He foreordained for each of us His children. God wants all to be saved, this is why he graciously waits upon us. He wants everyone to come to *repentance*. God draws men unto Himself. We are saved through God's grace when we respond in faithful obedience to His word that draws us to God (see Matthew 7:21 (KJV). Not everyone that saith unto me, Lord, Lord, shall enter into the kingdom of heaven; but he that doeth the will of my Father which is in heaven. God is always ready for men to repent and obey Acts 17:30 (NIV). In the past God overlooked such ignorance, but now he commands all people everywhere to repent. It is those who will do so that God has predestined for *salvation* I Thessalonians 5:9 (KJV). Praise God that He has not appointed us to His wrath, but has delivered us from it by the precious blood of Jesus. But it is up to us as to whether we will trust and obey just as I did that day in the closet.

...For we are his workmanship, created in Christ Jesus unto good works, which God hath before ordained that we should walk in them.... Ephesians 2:10 (NIV).

With a heart of joy,
With eyes that shine,
With a song of love,
With a purpose divine...

God's presence is within our body. He speaks to us and tells us what to do. With a whisper, reading the word, whispering through someone else to help or tell us. All of a sudden at times within pops up a dawning and you say to yourself Oh, yeah. A quick spontaneous combustion moves in. At times when I can't remember for a moment I stop and whisper a prayer to God for a second my memory comes right back and I remember.

God loves us - He loves us the same yesterday, today, and tomorrow. He has a future for each of us to accomplish in this life. Let's prepare ourselves in our own unique way and give our life to Him.

'SERENITY'

One early morning I was getting ready to go fishing with my brother-in-law. He had told me we will need to get up early and leave by 5:30am. When we arrived on the river the sun was rising over the water withdrawing the fog from the surface of the water. It was so pretty watching the fog rise up and go away with the sun. The light came in slowly upon us. It was the most peaceful moments of my life.

"In silence I see Him"

I wouldn't have reached a place where I found myself fully without God's *grace.*

'GOD WHISPERS IN SILENCE'

God is found in Silence

To search is the very reason why I write Whispers of God to a Hungry Heart for I know that life is a continuous search. I may not know all the answers all I know is God is real and he lives within my soul.

As we journey through life, things happen and we don't understand, perhaps we are not supposed to understand, we're just supposed to have faith and let it happen. We speak words at a moment not realizing it was for a future moment.

I have had two incidences where I spoke of angels and both times it was to a lady who would not be with us soon. Not knowing their purpose in life was finished. God speaks through us at times for the future…. such as speaking about angels when we are ready to leave this earth. God prepared the two ladies for their departure.

Words echo through the universe. God's Words upholds the universe by the word of his power.

God is always with us for He did not want us to doubt. He wants us to *believe,* to hope, to love and to see life the way he made it. Every time I begin to feel that there is no more strength in me, I always end up knowing that there is more in Him. I learned that everything has a purpose – the Bible says, "...but let God transform you inwardly by complete change of mind and heart then you will be able to know the will of God". Romans 12:2 (GNB). We begin to realize how special we are to God through His graces without asking. We can choose what is best for us – God comes into our hearts and we are guided by the wisdom of God. Abraham Lincoln was right when he said: "We are as happy as we decide to be." Furthermore, happiness is built through the foundation of life to praise, reverence, as we serve God. We must have the solitude in our hearts to attend to the invitation of the whisper of silence. *Peace* cannot be found outside ourselves but within and with God. It is in sharing that our life begins to find its true meaning. Where we choose to give our life is where God is calling us? God's grace and in the *whispers* of our heart. I Thank God that brought changes in my life and gave me the enlightenment I am searching for. God nurtured my spirit and watered the seed of my vocation for I am now ready to grow and have the courage to say Yes, Lord!

'TEACH ME, LORD'

What I don't know.
Show me which way
And speak within my soul...

Did I sign-up for transformation finding my 'pathway in life'? Do we have a level of caring and compassion that is all too rare? Every life that we touch is enhanced by letting our faith guide us. The process of writing a life script alone will bring opportunities to anyone. We are essentially changing our focus towards what we desire and away from what is wrong with our life.

I am reminded of a little song I learned as a little girl Into My Heart.

INTO MY HEART

Come into my heart, Lord Jesus.

"I desire to do your will, my God; your law is within my heart." Psalm 40:8 (NIV).

'GOD SPEAKS'...

erhaps we have been trusting God for something and it does not seem forthcoming. Have we went an extra step by fasting with our prayer, and gone to different mountains to seek God's face. Do we feel like we have done all within our power to accelerate our desire of change. Yet, the answer seems delayed and it's as if God has gone on vacation. This can cause weariness of the soul. Scripture has rightly stated that; hope deferred makes the heart sick ... Proverbs 13:12 (NIV).

So, if our heart is sick due to deferred hope, know that you are not alone. Others have experienced the same thing and some are still experiencing it.

'KNOWING'

Back about eight years ago I was fasting I was needing help in a situation. At the end of my fast I felt to keep fasting not for myself but for my family my fast shifted. My heart turned very heavy not knowing what was wrong. So, I interceded with fasting for a week or so for the members of my family and my friend David tuned in and was fasting with me for my family. I believe the fasting was for the future not for immediate of time. My grief had risen from the very depths of my soul. The glitter for fasting for my loved ones I knew not why? My heart during fasting drew in humility nearer to the heart of God. I made a sanctuary corner in my home devoted with dedication and reading God's words during fasting. I felt humble and felt near to the Father, His presence was strong at this particular time. I was trying to see the future holding on to hope and joy. During this time my joy dropped and I felt my joy was depleted my heart was so heavy. I could barely get out of bed a heavy burden came upon me. I whispered to God and said, "Where is my joy Lord?" I was stretching my legs trying to get out of bed my legs felt so heavy? I am in the kitchen putting dishes away and I opened the cabinet/cupboard my hands had frozen in place on the cupboard as sleeping. A voice came forth within and said, stop Glenda where is your joy? I started crying and I said. "Lord I don't know tell me, "He said the Joy is knowing all is well within your soul you are aligned with the Lord." Tears started flowing and I started weeping heavily my heart was overwhelmed of the presence of the Lord.

If your heart is heavy and you feel nothing is coming forth try to fast for the purpose of sincerity to the Lord. He will draw near to you.

Be truly *glad*.
There is wonderful
Joy ahead.
I Peter 1:6 (NLT).

May you have a day filled with *love* and laughter.

'EVERYWHERE'

God is everywhere. We do not need to be in a room full of people to get God to come. There is no place where a believer can get away from God's reach. His presence may be experienced at any time and at any place. When both of my daughters were born as soon as I reached my destination at home I had taken each baby and held her next to my breast. I whispered unto the Lord and I dedicated each child to His service. Asking His protection to guide each one in His light that He would watch over them when I was not around. Knowing God would take care of my children I felt comfort and peace. I am to love my God with all of me.

In the multitude of my thoughts within me thy comforts delight my soul. Psalm 94:19 (KJV).

God desires that his children are dedicated into faithfully serving him. How we treat the God who gave us life (and keeps on giving) should not be casual. As we devote our time and services to him, great and mighty works of God will manifest in our lives.

PRAYER

Dear God, thank You for the commitment You gave us to serve you; we will serve You always. Thank You for Your grace and empowerment to faithfully follow you, so that we can prosper in all our ways. For in the name of Jesus Christ we pray. amen.

I thank my God every time I remember you. Philippians 1:3 (NIV).

You are beautiful In God's eyes.

'PROTECTION'

One time at twenty six years old. I was riding this one evening on this stretch of highway I believe Route 2. I was riding to Curtice, Ohio. The person driving was going 80-100 mph. I closed my eyes and *whispered* a prayer and said, *"Lord, do you see me I need to make it to my destination I need your hedge of protection."* All at once it felt like we hydroplaned straight into the driveway safe. But, the very next evening this person was driving the same stretch of highway and he wrecked the truck straight into a ditch. I believe God heard my whisper of prayer and saved me that particular evening with His protection.

God has appointed each to its season. Each season is to be considered as part of a whole.

May the Lord look over us all, and guide us towards safe harbors. When we are in need of *protection for physical safety, God promises to be our provider* and strength!

THE LIGHT OF GOD

The light of God surrounds us,
The love of God enfolds us,
The power of God protects us...

'PURPOSEFUL'

When the testing of life feels like rushing uncontrollably down a river of despair, cling to the presence and purposefulness of God. This is not an accident, and we are not alone. You are not abandoned. God is with us in this chasm, for his glory and our good. Even in our darkest times, God is guiding us forward.

I walk old paths no more; the paths I travel now are new, where love abides and peace resides; Dear Christ, I've come to You.

'HEALING CAME SPEEDILY'

One day at work I receive this call and it was my boyfriend stating he was 'very sick'. At lunch I drove to him since he was seven miles away. I walk in the bedroom and he is in deep sweats. His mouth had thrush. He was feeling very lousy. I didn't want to leave him looking and feeling this way. So we talked and I tried to cool him down with a wet cloth. Then he said, "Will you whisper a prayer over me?" My heart tuned in heavily as I prayed. We both believing to receive. As soon as the prayer was over. His sweats disappeared. His face that was flush disappeared and the thrush disappeared. Healing came speedily.

Then shall your light break forth like the dawn, and your healing shall spring up speedily; your righteousness shall go before you; the glory of the Lord shall be your rear guard. Exodus 15:26 (ESV).

God's ear is listening for my call,
He's there to help me if I ask.
I Bless Thee while I Live: I will Lift up my
Hands in Thy Name.

And the prayer offered in faith will make the sick person well; the Lord will raise them up. If they have sinned, they will be forgiven. James 5:15,16 (NIV).

I desire to be right with God so when I pray my prayer is powerful and effective and I know my prayer makes it through to the throne of God.

'NOT KNOWING'

I was raised in a minister's home my dad was a Church of God/Pentecostal minister very strict. I could not wear pants until I was fourteen years old. We wore dresses all the time. Our home was a very calm home never no arguing. My mother had taken care of six children and made sure the house was well kept, our clothes always clean and dinner was always on the table. We never went out to eat. My mother was a good southern cook. I was the youngest of the six and look at or observe attentively what my older siblings were doing. My mom spent a lot of time with the older siblings. We never went to a doctor nor a dentist. We were never sick or had a tooth problem. I decided I was going to visit Plan Parenthood. I made my way downtown to visit and received a packet of birth controls. After watching my two sisters get pregnant. I was determined I was not going allow that to happen to me. I tucked my packet of birth controls in my drawer for the future. All the children moved out of the house everyone went their way. I was the last child. I enrolled in an all girl school. My parents decided to move and it was far away from my school. I decided to hitch-hike to school. I couldn't drive. I was fifteen years old two months shy of being sixteen. I came home one day from school and my mother was very upset and told me to get my suitcase and get out? I didn't know what was going on and did not know the reason why? So, I get my suitcase together with some of my clothes and left all my memorabilia and the rest of my stuff etc. at home. My mother and father bought a new double wide trailer near the border line of Michigan. I am walking in the snow outside not knowing where I was headed or where I was going and did not know the reason why? My brother came and found me and told me why she kicked me out of the house? The reason was she found my birth controls in my drawer. My mother and mine relationship was never mended and we never had a relationship from that time forward. She never tried to be in my life. In the later years I did receive birthday cards. I made many whispering prayers during this time. I did not attend her funeral…

Whether we have had a personal relationship with God for years or we are only beginning to discover who Jesus is, we all need guidance sometimes when it comes to our personal life prayers. It's often hard to find the words to pray during a crisis.

At times we need a prayer for peace.

PRAYER FOR PEACE

Father God, our heart is filled with chaos with fear and confusion. We feel as if we are drowning. We need the strength and peace that only You can give. Right now, we choose to rest in You. Many may need You at this time bless them and help them in their time of need. Thank You, In Christ Jesus I pray, amen.

Lord, when our heart is broken You are near.
Our spirit is crushed, but You are our rescuer.
Your Word is our *hope*.
It revives us and comforts us especially now.

OH GOD, HOW 'MIGHTY' YOU ARE!!

Mighty, everlasting Father, we bow down before Your throne of grace and mercy. We bless Your Holy name, as we surrender our praise to You our loving king. We can rest assured that we are fully protected and saved. We cling to our Jesus, Every moment, every day; Yes, He is our life, Our purposeful pathway.

FEAR OF THE LORD

To respect God's majesty

Lord, the gods of other religions are not approachable. You are the one true Living God, a loving heavenly Father. You say we can come before you with confidence. You hear our prayers. You know our heart. Thank you, for speaking to our heart. We praise You in Your name amen.

…' he hears us '. I John 5:14 NIV.

'GOD DELIVERS'

I am sharing with you to let you know God is an awesome God! My husband lost his job and so he decided to take on construction work freely for himself (self-employed) and he hired men to help him. He had underbid a few jobs because he was depending on the men's expertise and in the middle of the jobs the men were slacking and not doing their job when Patrick had to leave and go get materials. When Patrick found out he had to fire these men. In the meantime, a few of the jobs weren't completely done in the way Patrick wanted the work to be performed so he had taken it upon himself and redo some of the work with whispers of prayer on my part. The jobs had taken much longer and the work went under as far as the money is concerned. In the ending part the saw went through Patrick's leg and had to be rushed to the emergency room he had stitches inside and out. It was one eighth of an inch from his artery - very bad deep wound in his leg. In the meantime I receive a letter inside my door stating they are putting the house up for sale and we have to be out by December. So, Patrick is in desperation needing money and trying to finish these jobs by himself. I start fasting and whispering prayer heavier Oh, God deliver us and help us. In the meantime, we can't have the heat turned on in the house and I am freezing, and we barely have enough money for food and we have to save money to move? Patrick grabs a steady job as a superintendent over a stable construction company. In the meantime, I have all my stuff in storage and it is behind eight hundred dollar. The storage is scheduled to be auctioned off Nov 18th and I have every bit of my life in this storage. Patrick was in Home Depot and this man came up to him and started talking to him and he wanted Patrick to go to his house to do a few odd jobs. The man said, "Patrick I am your angelic being to help you, what can I do for you?" So, Patrick told him the mess we were in and the man volunteered and paid our storage for us. What an awesome Father! So, now Patrick has a steady job, my storage has been paid but, still we are in trouble because I am packing and have nowhere to go and have very little money. We are waiting on God's deliverance. Waiting on God's help is a test of our own seeking his face and waiting for the outcome. I tell this story to let you know of our awesome Father who hears our whispering voice of His children. God held me in peace in my heart in time of trouble and he delivered and rescued us. My storage was paid, Patrick received an awesome job, we did move into a townhouse and did not have to pay deposit. Oh, God you are so good! Trust in God in all things and He will deliver you!

I feel like a pioneer; with hopes and disappointments, struggles and triumphs our independence and skills wanting to work freely, learning patience and perseverance overcoming many obstacles, hardships and tragedy; and we entered into **Victory**.

I recall the song of **Victory in Jesus**

'SADNESS'

My daughter and I was having a nice day the end of April/94 (she pumped my gas for the first time) and was feeling a little bit older she was fourteen years old two months she would have been fifteen years old. Aleisha and I were talking about how angels come to be with someone when they die. My aunt had just passed away the end of March and this was the end of April and we were conversing about how one dies and how the angels come forth to meet you and take you away. She was looking forward to go to the cinema that night I said, "I will take you do you have a ride back?" She said, "No problem mom I have a ride." So, she was getting ready and standing at my bedroom door watching me get dressed and I said, "You know Aleisha if you were to die your stuff will go to Heidi and vice versa." She said, "Yes I know mom." I had taken her to the cinema and it was getting late I was wondering where she was? I fell asleep and I woke up at 4:00am and she wasn't home? At 7:00am the police came to my door and holding her necklace and he said, "Are you familiar with this necklace?" I said, "Its Aleisha's necklace." He said, "Well I hate to inform you but your daughter was just in a car accident this morning around 4:08am and she is dead her neck was broken in a car accident." I immediately try to recall our conversation for that day in my mind and the conversation was about angels. God prepared for this event knowing it was going to take place. I know our conversation was about angels and God covered my heart for the preparation. The time arrived for the angels to take her home. This is how God prepares conversation for the future.

The boy giving Aleisha and her friend a ride home was twenty one years old. He had taken a new medication for a collapse lungs chasing it down with a beer right before the ride. This was April 30th when the girls came out of the cinema when he decided to take the girls for a thrill ride in the Old Town Buford, GA by a railroad track. A straight street where kids speed down the road with smooth bumps for thrills. So, he takes them to the street and charges down the road and hits one of the bumps and they went up in the air and he lost control came down and hit a culvert and bounced back out came straight down and hit a big oak tree. Aleisha my daughter was in the front seat and her neck was broken instantly. But, her friend was hiding behind Aleisha in the back seat and was protected, she scrapped her way out of the back seat over this guy and Aleisha. She screamed for help and someone heard her and came running and she was placed in the hospital. The guy was not hurt. They had taken him to court but with his medical condition they didn't put him in jail they gave him five years house arrest. I called the hospital to talk to Aleisha's friend but, she wouldn't talk. The person in her room told me she was going to be in a wheel chair for a long time? The boy called my house to tell me he was sorry and was sobbing. I was tongued tied and I didn't know what to say except thank you for calling that is nice of you. I did not know Aleisha's friend. I went to the junk yard to see the car and the car was completely totaled a small mustang. Aleisha was an Amazon girl and that car would had squashed her.

Sadness/fear came over me my joy and happiness disappeared. I was so distraught it felt like the house had a feeling of hopelessness. I went around the house proclaiming God in every room because fear entered into my being. I quit work knowing it wasn't important. I went back to school for three to four years and received my Associate degree LAN – Local Area Network certified Administrator. I started searching and pulled out all my Bible's and dictionaries in search of our souls where do we go? I studied from the time she left me May 1st 1994 through Spring, Summer, Fall and Winter till the next Spring. I was in total desperation feeling lost.

When my daughter die they told me if a rescue squad didn't get to the individual within fourteen minutes the person is likely to die. My heart was already broken and to hear this made it even worse. So as I traveled and I would hear a 'siren' it broke my heart I would burst out crying and gushing of tears I would pull over to the side of the road. I would intercede and pray for the person who was in need of rescue. This went on for many years. Everyone of us have some kind of flashback in our lives. But you know God heals broken hearts.

When I was sad and tearful I would call out to the Lord whispering many prayers and asked for God's help. I started lighting candles throughout the house. I would repeat a verse I found in the Bible "Trust in the Lord with all your heart, And lean not on your own understanding; In all your ways acknowledge Him, And He shall direct your paths." Proverbs 3:5-6 (NKJV) I would light the candles ritually repeat this verse many times throughout the day…til this day I light a candle.

'TRUST'

When I was in great pain of my deceased daughter of fourteen yrs old I was in devastation. I did not know how to react or show my feelings and I was stone cold. I had taken up the verse Trust in the Lord lean not on your own understanding acknowledge God and he will direct your path.' Proverbs 3:5-6 (NIV). I started whispering prayers asking God to help me to understand constantly. So, every day I would light a candle and state this verse and cry to God. I had been praying and my body felt so heavy and overloaded and I couldn't function mentally nor physically. I went to church one Sunday morning in need of relief. My husband and my daughter went with me to a charismatic church called River of Life in Lilburn, Georgia. The minister asked the congregation to open our hands and stretch them out to God while standing. I was in despair and at my limit and I started gushing and crying to God. *I said, "Lord I can't take this pain please take this heavy pain that I am feeling [away]."* As I lift my hands direct into the air and said, "Lord I am trusting in you and you said if I Trust in the Lord lean not on my own understanding and acknowledge You - You will direct my path". As soon as I said these words tingles came forth at the top of my head tingling like a fine mist straight down through my body. Pushing heaviness throughout my fingertips and throughout my toes. The heaviness that I was feeling completely left my body like turning on/off of a light switch. I was healed. My countenance of heaviness left, relief came forth with joy it felt like light overcame darkness. Despair had to leave. The heaviness of the darkness was leaving lighter and lighter I was feeling as it was leaving my body. Joy came forth and my face felt like I had taken off a mask. Depression left. ***I call this a Miracle.***

When hard pressed, I cried to the LORD; he brought me into a spacious place. Psalm 118:5 (NIV).

God gives us extra energy when we had none. I was given an extra dose of energy where I had none.

That energy is God's energy, an energy deep within you, God himself willing and working at what will give him the most pleasure. Do everything readily and cheerfully - no bickering, no second-guessing allowed! Go out into the world uncorrupted, a breath of fresh air in this squalid and polluted society. Provide people with a glimpse of good living and of the living God. Philippians 2:13-23 (MSG).

'BEING KIND'

When I was much younger and I was trying to be nice and useful. I met an elderly Greek nationality man I am guessing around eighty years old. He lived down the street from me maybe five blocks or so. We met in a restaurant near my home. We talked and became friends. I would walk down the street to his house and visit him. He was a lonely man. I would sit on his front porch and chat with him. He eventually gave me his deceased wife's 'Currier and Ives' dish set and two Germany platters. He kept calling me and I was busy tending to my flowers, I had taken up piano lessons, I bought an AKC Doberman etc. Finally I told Jim I will come his way with my dog but it was weeks later that I finally went. I had made a loaf of butter nut bread and I said to myself old man Jim would like this. I proceeded to walk to his house to give him the bread and to chat with him. I arrive at his house and he was not around. I was wondering if he was back in the nursing home a few blocks away? I checked the nursing home and they said he wasn't there. I went back to his house and left the butter nut bread behind his screened front door and went home. I walked back there the next day and I see the butter nut bread was still there. I was looking up at his house and thinking where is he it was a very small cracker box home? A lady next door came out on her porch and she said, "Are you looking for Jim?" I said, yes. She said, "Oh he died last week."

Taking time for others is important my heart was broken. We should sparkle kindness to others every chance we get.

Being kind to family is natural and being kind to friends can be a necessity but, being kind to strangers is an act that will set us apart.

Dear God, let me be kind and loving to inspire just one at a time.

'INSPIRATION RADIANCE'

I met this elderly lady and she was very eccentric and her radiance shined through her personality. I talked with her many times. Then she invited me to her home. She lived in Michigan. From my house it was about forty five minutes to one hour away. Because of her radiance I was happy she invited me. She inspired my heart without even trying. She was an elderly lady that had big faith, she whispered prayers to me to bless me.

This one particular day I told her I will come to visit her. I arrive at her house it was a tiny house. She had a husband/boyfriend I don't know which. I didn't pry into her business. They had a huge garden and gathered up many vegetables. As I entered into her house she told me she had no one to do her hair. I volunteered to do her hair for her. As I was doing her hair she tells me what an artist she is. In her sunroom I am guessing maybe 30 or more paintings/drawings. She had them covered with canvas. Her sweet personality covered her soul with brightness she barely could see but she still was drawing in her early eighties. She inspired my life with her beauty. She lived as if she had nothing but her Spirit said otherwise. She was a mother/grandmother who had open arms for everyone. I still think of her from time to time and think how she influenced my heart with such beauty. "A thing of beauty is a joy forever: Its loveliness increases".

Your adornment must not be *merely* external—braiding the hair, and wearing gold jewelry, or putting on dresses; but *let it be* the hidden person of the heart, with the imperishable quality of a gentle and quiet spirit, which is precious in the sight of God. I Peter 3:3-4 (NIV).

'DREAMS SUSTAIN'

ne time I was in deep despair after my daughter had died. My boyfriend and I had broken up after seven years. I was very sad. I had just bought a house and I was raking leaves and talking to the Lord. I felt complete talking to God. I was telling him how sad I was and I needed his help over my situation. My boyfriend wanted to get married and I didn't want to. At least I thought I didn't want to. I told God I needed him to de-clutter my life. I was crying and it was late at night and I was heading to bed my heart was heavy. As I went to sleep I was feeling abandoned. I went to sleep and fell into a deep deep dream that last all night. In my dream I had met this man that was a lawyer and he was showing me his house. He had a beautiful home I was admiring his statues, fireplace, the volume/space of the rooms he was showing me. He was attentive to me with gracefulness. He was a very handsome gentleman, intelligent and kind. The warm inviting home had my interest in many ways. When I had awaken I felt complete, no sadness, no abandonment, satisfied and my feelings were put back together as if nothing had happened. I felt a fear of inadequacy. The fear of inadequacy carries the power to paralyze, but we can move beyond it to embrace life fully as God intends. God gave me a dream for completeness… long story short Patrick and I then went to the court house and we were married. We knew to be blessed we had to be married.

When ideas are impossible then we should know it came from God. He gives us ideas, rewards and opportunities. He implants upon our hearts. God had put my heart back together where it belonged.

Occasionally God nudges us to do something far beyond our comfort zone.

The truth is, God often invites us to do things far beyond our natural capabilities so we can grow in our understanding of His character. We find courage to say yes by filling our minds with His truth: For I can do everything with the help of Christ who gives me strength. Philippians 4:13 (NIV).

Admitting our fear is another step toward freedom. The Old Testament tells the story of King Jehoshaphat feeling *afraid* as war approached. He admitted his feelings and dependency upon God:

See II Chronicles 20:12 (NASB) For we are powerless before this great multitude who are coming against us; nor do we know what to do, but our eyes are on You.

Jehoshaphat humbled himself before God by admitting his dependence upon Him. But he didn't stop there. He took another important step by moving into battle despite those *fears*. And what happened? God honored him for trusting Him. He experienced God's strength at work on his behalf.

NOW I AWAKE AND
SEE THE LIGHT

The Lord has kept me through trying times. To Thee I lift my voice and pray and Thank Him for this day.

'GOD LISTENS'

One time my husband and I worked together for this storage company. One morning we came in to work and our checks were waiting on us to be let go. The company decided to downsize. We had til the week-end to get moved. We were living at the storage facility as a fringe benefit. We didn't know where to go. I had saved up some money in which I had tucked away. We moved in with my sister who was in a bad situation but, we didn't know it when we moved in. After we moved in she was behind on a few things and had to be moving out after two months we were there. So now, there is three of us needing a place to lay our heads. I started leaning and whispering to God for help. We are in our vehicle and looking for a place to stay and my sister's friend told us about a house that was for rent. We went over to this house and it was an old house that was built in the 1930's with a tin roof. We inquired about the house and I told the man we needed a place ASAP. He said he had a lady who was in line to rent the house. She had steady income coming in monthly through social security and he would rather rent to her. We left our name and number and went on way. In the middle of the day and we had came up with nothing. I whispered a prayer "Oh, Lord please help us find a home." I was earnest with my prayer. We stopped to eat and went in Del Taco. I left my phone in the car. Our only conversation was what are we going to do? I am whispering heavier to God for help. When we arrived back into the car I had a message on my phone. It was the gentleman who wanted to rent to this lady. He stated the application failed. He said he would consider us to rent the house. We were so relieved knowing God saw and knew our situation and helped us when we were in dire straights in need.

We all are faced with trying times. Our Father in heaven remains the same, regardless of shifting circumstances in our lives. When we are hard-pressed, we look to Him for stability and direction. Through Christ, love flows through us, especially in times when we find ourselves struggling. If I can have forgiveness, and if I can have the promise of omnipotent help from Jesus who is the same yesterday today and forever my heart will be strong, and I will be able to carry on another day.

Every good and perfect gift is from above, coming down from the Father of the heavenly lights, who does not change like shifting shadows. James 1:17 (NIV).

'PRAYER'

...hope

Heavenly father, we are your humble servants,
We come before you today in need of hope,
We are faced with trying times. Allow your love
to flow through us. Do not let shifting shadows
of circumstances over whelm us. Allow your
peace to sustain us in your name Jesus we pray. amen.

SPECIAL MOMENT
OF WHISPERS OF PRAYER

My earthly father taught a few prayers and I am making sure my daughter 'Heidi' remember a few as well. In Deuteronomy 6 God reveals why He commands parents to be fruitful—not just to have children, but godly children who will pass a godly legacy by connecting one generation to the next. The home is the best place for a child to learn about God. At dinner time I had Heidi to repeat after me and this is the prayer I had her memorize....

Now unto him that is able to keep you from falling, and to present you faultless before the presence of his glory with exceeding joy, to the only wise God our Saviour, be glory and majesty, dominion and power both now and forever. amen. Jude 1:24-25 (NASB).

It is important to pass legacy of God's word to our children. Heidi is grown now and on her own. But the legacy of whispered prayer is stationary.

Tell it to your children, and let your children tell it to their children, and their children to the next generation. Joel 1:3 (NIV).

It is amazing to me how many people can not quote The Lord's prayer. The Lord's prayer Jesus taught to us to show us how to pray. Jesus Christ gave us a pattern or model for prayer. It teaches us how to approach God in prayer. It starts out Our Father who Art in Heaven. He is our Father, and we are his humble children. We have a close bond. As a *heavenly*, perfect Father, we can trust that he loves us and will listen to our prayers. The use of Our in the prayer reminds us that we (his followers) are all part of the same family of God.

PRAYER

MATTHEW 6:9 (KJV)
Our Father which Art in Heaven

Our Father which art in heaven,
Hallowed be thy name.
Thy kingdom come,
Thy will be done
In earth, as it is in heaven.
Give us this day

Our daily bread.
And forgive us our debts,
As we forgive our debtors.
And lead us not into temptation,
But deliver us from evil:
For thine is the kingdom, and the power,
and the glory, for ever.
amen.

I had Heidi my daughter to memorize Our Father who Art in Heaven. It was important for me to instill godly virtues in her. When I held her close to my breast after birth I told God she is His. Ever since she was a child she had interest in God. I did the right thing to teach her a few prayers but God did the rest. He came within her heart as a child and she had taken upon herself to visit a church close near our residence.

UNDERSTANDING

To grasp faith's mysteries

P raying in a private place. But you, when you pray, go into your room, and when you have shut your door, pray to your Father who is in the secret place; and your Father who sees in secret will reward you Matt. 6:6 (NKJV). If we are really serious about finding a quiet area to be alone with the Lord in prayer, He will provide one. The Father, who sees what is done in secret, will reward us. It may require a little creativity and adjustment on our part, but God wants to meet with each of us privately so we can develop an intimate relationship with Him.

'INTO MY HEART'
Come into my heart, Lord Jesus.

When I was whispering and searching God's word one of the great words he had given me was:

'SELL ALL YOU HAVE AND GIVE TO THE POOR'
'if you want to be perfect'...

The Promise of Treasure in Heaven: "Jesus said to him, "If you want to be perfect, go, sell what you have and give to the poor, and you will have Treasure in heaven, and come, Follow Me." Matt 19:21 (NIV).

Note: In the Mediterranean world, to sell all would mean to sale of the family home and land. This would mean a rejection of his identity as defined by his position and his family's in the community. To Reject his family in favor of a relationship with Jesus and surrogate family formed Jesus' followers! The wealthy young man turned away regretfully, unwilling to make this kind of sacrifice, even for a place and treasure in the world to come. Jesus had an unique purpose in view in presenting this young man with this dilemma. Jesus has already asked the man if he had kept his commandments, and he quoted only from the second tablet of the Law which only dealt with human interpersonal relationships, and the young man said he kept these laws. Jesus told the young man to sell all and follow Him, the focus shifted to the First Tablet of the Law, which governs relationship with God. Jesus, Himself the God in whom the young man, believed, gave him a command. Go and sell, and follow me. And that command was disobeyed! The young man's response revealed that His Heart was far from God. In a choice between wealth and Jesus, money won. In choosing wealth, the young man broke first and greatest of the commandments---to have no other God than the one supreme Lord. The incident was an effort by Jesus to reveal to the young man his lostness it was also, a warning to us that

NOTHING MUST BE ALLOWED to take Christ's Place in our HEARTS.

'WHY JESUS FOLDED THE BURIAL CLOTH AFTER HIS RESURRECTION?'

The Gospel of John 20:7 (KJV) tells us that the napkin, which was placed over the face of Jesus, was not just thrown aside like the grave clothes. The Bible takes an entire verse to tell us that the napkin was neatly folded, and was placed separate from the grave clothes.

...

Early Sunday morning, while it was still dark, Mary Magdalene came to the tomb and found that the stone had been rolled away from the entrance. She ran and found Simon Peter and the other disciple, the one whom Jesus loved. She said, 'They have taken the Lord's body out of the tomb, and I don't know where they have put him!' Peter and the other disciple ran to the tomb to see. The other disciple outran Peter and got there first. He stooped and looked in and saw the linen cloth lying there, but he didn't go in. Then Simon Peter arrived and went inside. He also noticed the linen wrappings lying there, while the cloth that had covered Jesus' head was folded and laying to the side. Was that important? Absolutely!

Is it really significant? Yes!

In order to understand the significance of the folded napkin, you have to understand a little bit about Hebrew tradition of that day. The folded napkin had to do with the Master and Servant, and every Jewish boy knew this tradition. When the servant set the dinner table for the master, he made sure that it was exactly the way the master wanted it. The table was furnished perfectly, and then the servant would wait, just out of sight, until the master had finished eating, and the servant would not dare touch that table, until the master was finished. Now, if the master were done eating, he would rise from the table, wipe his fingers, his mouth, and clean his beard, and would wad up that napkin and toss it onto the table. The servant would then know to clear the table. For in those days, the wadded napkin meant, I'm done. But if the master got up from the table, and folded his napkin, and laid it beside his plate, the servant would not dare touch the table, because the folded napkin meant, I'm coming back!

Jesus is COMING BACK!!!

I love when God shows us new things. These words I was not brought up with. The words are from the Lord in quiet chambers of research.

This is what my Lord is doing I ask, seek and knocked and I received...

RED LIKE CRIMSON

Put me in remembrance; let us contend together; state your case, that you may be acquitted.... Isaiah 43:26 (NKJV). (there is forgiveness with God, and shows the freeness of Divine mercy).

The **Promise**: Though your sins are like scarlet, they shall be white as snow; though they are red like crimson, they shall be as wool Isa 1:18 (NKJV) Isaiah's first sermon is an indictment of God's people as evildoers. Yet God calls His people back to Him and promises that they can be cleansed. The reference to *scarlet* and *crimson* is significant. Many of the ancient dyes did not fix well, and so faded. But crimson/scarlet dyes were the most permanent known in the ancient world. (scarlet and other bright shades of red are the colors most associated with courage, force, passion, heat, and joy) scarlet has been a color of power, wealth and luxury. Scarlet is the color worn by a cardinal, and is associated with the blood of Christ and the Christian martyrs, and with sacrifice. What a stunning promise---that God is able to make the permanently stained white as snow! Yet promise of forgiveness and cleansing from sin is extended throughout scripture to all people on the basis of faith!

With Faith God Promises Forgiveness!
Our Faith is being Obedient to God.

Review the past for me, let us argue the matter together; state the case for your innocence. Isaiah 43:26 (NIV).

"Put me in remembrance; let us contend together'; state your case, that you may be acquitted." Just as a good defense attorney can possibly win a case with a good, convincing, closing argument before a jury – so can we if we have good enough reasons and contentions to present before the Lord on whatever it is we are asking Him for. Praise God for what it is we are wanting and THANK HIM IN ADVANCE FOR HIS MERCY!

DECIDE WHAT IS RIGHT OR WRONG

Each Christian must decide what is right or wrong for him or her. Paul teaches that if you believe a particular action to be wrong for you, then it is wrong. He says in Romans 14:4 (NIV), "I know and am convinced in the Lord Jesus that nothing is unclean in itself; but to him who thinks anything to be unclean, to him it is unclean. He taught that **ALL THINGS WERE CLEAN**. In other words, there was no sin in eating meat sacrificed to ...idols (it was morally neutral). But he also teaches that if a person believes it is sinful to indulge in a practice, then it is indeed sinful for them.

EACH PERSON MUST BE FULLY CONVINCED IN HIS OWN MIND. If there is doubt, then it is better to refrain from participating rather than engaging in what has become a sinful action for the person. Doubt or uncertainty is a sufficient reason to refrain from a particular activity or behavior.

A key test of Christian obedience is whether a person can do so for the Lord. Whoever regards one day as special does so to the Lord. Whoever eats meat does so to the Lord, for they give thanks to God; and whoever abstains does so to the Lord and gives thanks to God Rom. 14:6 (NIV). Christians are to live for the Lord because we are the Lord's.

If we live, we live for the Lord; and if we die, we die for the Lord. So, whether we live or die, we belong to the Lord.. If one cannot participate in an activity while serving the Lord, then he or she should refrain. Rom. 14:8 (NIV).

But it would be wise not to participate publicly but privately for the sake of a believer who might be hurt by one's actions.

If your brother or sister is distressed because of what you eat, you are no longer acting in love. Do not by your eating destroy someone for whom Christ died. Romans 14:15 (NIV).

Know that the same spark of life that is within us, is within all of our animal friends, the desire to live is the same within all of us...

My heavenly Father, gave me many messages but these are the ones I cherish the most. *Remember God's Word.*

"Then the angel showed me a river with the water of life, clear as crystal, flowing from the throne of God and of the Lamb." Revelation 22:1 (NLT).

WALKING IN THE REALM

In the Will of God is like being in the center of a fast flowing river.

In the center of the river the flow is strongest and fastest. The further away from the center of the river we drift, the slower and less directed the flow. We're still in the flow, but it's not as strong or sure.

In the center of God's Will, His guidance is strongest and most sure. But the further away from the center of God's Will we drift, the slower we move, and the guidance, direction, and protection we would have received from Him is weaker and less effective, almost indiscernible. We move from His *Perfect Will* into His *Permissive Will*, and then out of His Will altogether.
Wading to the edge of the river, we eventually step out and find our self on the shore of our pride and independence, and the river flows on without us. Likewise, stepping out of God's Will, we are on our own, left to our own devices as the will of God moves on without us. Out of the river, we try to make our way, but it's more difficult to move forward, because there are obstacles.

We try to move parallel to the river, keeping it in sight, but there are obstacles in the path, forcing movement around them. This causes us to travel in a different direction than the river, which is now so far away that it can't even be seen. Trying to serve or even follow God when we are out of His Will becomes frustrating because of the obstacles that force movement further away from God's plan for our life. Bad relationships, wrong career choice, poor health, lack of education, and finances are only some of the wrong roads on which we might find our self. Subsequently, our life ends up on a wrong path or stuck at a dead end going nowhere and we step out of the aroma of the *Protection of God*.

Now, we could make our way back to where we left the river of God's will, try to reenter, and find the place that was originally meant for us, but that's not always practical. Maybe our spot in the river has already moved on, or our place was filled with another. Do not Despair! There is another place for us in the river. God's Will and plan for our life yet waits! Make our way directly to the river of God's Will at whichever point along life's journey we now find our self.

Get back to the center of the river

This is the story of my (friend 'David's' quest) for spirituality.

David's Quest... David was a man from Oklahoma and he 'hitch hiked' to Mississippi. He got himself in a lot of trouble in earlier years and lost his driver's license. When he was in jail he became a Christian. He was involved with prison ministry. So, David decided to go to school for prison ministry. When he was dismissed from jail he had new goals in life and one of them was prison ministry. He had taken up contracting work because he was very handy with his hands and knew how to build things.

He had a side ministry where he would go to the ocean and pick up stones and place them in a necklace setting. He would bless them and send them out to people. The stones were very pretty. He would go to the gulf line of Texas to pick these stones up. He and his mother knew how to create beautiful jewelry. But he will give them away to people who needed God's blessings. He would pray over them and send them out to others. David was having a hard time in life not having a license etc. So, he decided to go back to Oklahoma while in search of completing his prison ministry. While he was in Oklahoma he decided to go to Lodi, California to a big church he had great dreams of attending. Hitch hiking on his way to California he slept under bridges because he was on foot. He carried a guitar with him because he loved to sing. He called out for help and asking me could I send him a few dollars. He indicated he needed shoes. So, Patrick went to Wal-mart to send him some money to get food, shoes and get a train ticket and place him on a train so that he can get to his destination. He arrives in California and very anxious to visit this big church in hopes of promoting a prison ministry. He now is communicating to us through the Library. He went inside this big church in need. He needed a place to lay his head while completing his prison ministry. He had great insights of faith in God with great intuition what he thought God wanted him to do. He is inside this church and received no help whatsoever from them 'they ignored him. He was devastated. He went to the park to sleep because he had nowhere to lay his head. He went into the library to communicate to us to tell us the story about the church. He went outside after talking to us and sat down by a big tree leaned on it and went to sleep and never woke up. I received contact from his mother to tell me what happened with him at the end. His story reminds me of Christ when Jesus replied,

"Foxes have dens, and birds of the air have nests, but the Son of Man has no place to lay His head." Matthew 8:20 (NIV).

Jesus made the point that there is a cost to following Him. The scribe who said he wanted to follow Jesus wherever He went was not considering the lifestyle Jesus led. Our Lord was functionally homeless; He and His disciples stayed in the homes of those who would take them in.

Our Responsibility for the Homeless

We have a responsibility to provide both physical and spiritual support to those in need. Also we have a duty to feed the hungry and to bless the poor. We also have a responsibility to provide shelter for those who are homeless. We have a duty to clothe those in need and to visit the sick. 'For I was hungry, and you gave Me *something* to eat; I was thirsty, and you gave Me *something* to drink; I was a stranger, and you invited Me in; naked, and you clothed Me; I was sick, and you visited Me; I was in prison, and you came to Me. Matthew 25:35, 36 (NIV).

Blessed are those whose help is the God of Jacob, whose hope is in the LORD their God. He is the Maker of heaven and earth, the sea, and everything in them- he remains faithful forever. He upholds the cause of the oppressed and gives food to the hungry. The LORD sets prisoners free. Psalm 146:5-7 (NASB).

Why do we *whisper* prayer?

God has called us into a relationship with himself. Relationships require communication. Prayer is communication between a holy God and beloved us. Throughout God's word we're taught the significance and role of *whispered prayer. God commands us to pray.*

Then you will call upon Me and come and pray to Me, and I will listen to you. You will seek Me and find *Me* when you search for Me with all your heart. Jeremiah 29:12,13 (NASB).

God wants to be in relationship with us. And He knows we need what He can give. Through prayer, we experience life transformation, life-renewing intimacy with the creator of the universe. *God reveals himself to us through prayer.*

"Teach me to do Your will, for You are my God. May Your gracious spirit lead me forward on a firm footing" (note: which is on a Level Ground). Psalm 143:10 (NIV).

We learn more and more about God's character and how His perfect will is working itself out in our own life. Deepening our understanding of God also deepens our faith and desire to worship. God invites us to bring our burdens and needs to Him in prayer.

"Come to Me, all of you who are Weary and Carry Heavy Burdens, and I will Give you Rest". Matthew 11:28 (NIV).

We have a Heavenly Father who is more than able to bring Victory to any challenge we face. God is a spiritual and physical healer. Like any healthy relationship, we must keep a line of communication open.

God responds to the *whisper* prayers of His people.

WHISPERS OF PRAYER

I t is through *whispers of prayer*, that God's work is accomplished on earth. The apostle Paul continually asked for prayer in his missionary endeavors and saw prayer as vital to his success. God imparts wisdom and understanding through prayer. "If we need Wisdom—if we want to know what God wants us to do—ask Him, and He will gladly tell us. He will not resent us from asking".

If any of you lacks wisdom, you should ask God, who gives generously to all without finding fault, and it will be given to you. James 1:5 (NIV).

As we become increasingly aware of our limitations, we can rest in the knowledge that our God is omniscient. Availing ourselves of God's counsel is a blessing of prayer. God exercises His authority and ability to do the impossible through the *prayers* of His people

"If you believe, you will receive whatever you ask for in prayer" Matthew 21:22 (NIV).

Our hearts pound with great confidence as we take mighty tasks to our exceedingly Mighty Lord. **God extends His power to us through** whispers of prayer so that we may resist bad influences. Keep alert and pray. Otherwise the bad influences will overpower us. For though the spirit is willing enough, the body is weak! With whispers of prayer, we always have a proven *shield of protection* available. Just say the word.

Watch and pray so that you will not fall into temptation. The spirit is willing, but the flesh is weak." Matthew 26:41 (NIV).

…The prayer of a righteous person is powerful and effective.. James 5:16 (NIV).

Our Father Prayer in Scripture. In Matthew 6:9-13 (KJV) and in Luke 11:2-4 (KJV) we find Jesus instructing his apostles how they should pray. This well known scripture is remembered as The Lord's Prayer, and also known by Our Father Prayer.

Did you know in The Lords Prayer that Hallowing be thy name means your name echo through the universe. This shows that prayers go on forever.

The word Hallowed means **sanctified** or **set apart for sacred use**.

God's name is never to be taken in vain. https://www.biblestudytools.com/bible-study/topical-studies/what-does-hallowed-be-thy-name-mean.html

The word hallowed God's name we are saying that his name is holy. But, to take things a little bit deeper, what does it really mean to be holy?

WHAT DOES IT MEAN TO BE HOLY?

According to Merriam Webster, to be holy is to be, "exalted or worthy of complete devotion as one perfect in goodness and righteousness." There is an aspect of perfection and worthiness involved, and each time we think of God's name as hallowed, it should bring us to consider his greatness and his majesty *in need of nothing.*

If God has no will then He would have no influence over the affairs of mankind, we would then be in charge which is not a comforting thought.

COUNSEL TO MAKE WISE DECISIONS

How then can we see through Gods eyes?
The answer is discernment. *Whispering Prayer* leads to discernment and discernment leads to action based on the discernment and without surrender, discernment is not possible. Without discernment AND action based on discernment Jesus cannot be Lord of our lives. If Jesus is not Lord of our lives, then holiness is not possible. Matthew 19:17-21 (NIV) When a rich young man came to Jesus, he asked Jesus what he has to do to possess eternal life. Jesus said, *If you wish to enter into life, keep the commandments.... commandments are our guideline.*

To be perfect, to live the life to the fullest - to please God, we have to detach ourselves from everything and follow Jesus. Jesus looks for *obedience.*

WHAT IS GOD'S WILL?

God First

I Thessalonians 5:18 (NIV) give thanks in all circumstances... I Peter 2:15 (NIV) For it is God's will that by doing 'good'.... Proverbs 3:5 (NIV) *Trust in the LORD with all your heart, and do not lean on your own understanding....* Philippians 2:13 (NIV) *For it is God who is at work in you, both to will and to work for His good purpose.* Romans 12:2 (NIV) Do not conform to the pattern of this world, but be transformed by the renewing of your mind. Then you will be able to test and approve what God's will is--his good, pleasing and perfect will.

JESUS SHARES HOW NOT TO PRAY

- We are to pray in secret –
- Jesus asks us to go to a private place since our heavenly Father already knows what we are going to pray about.
- Jesus tells us not to ramble on and on, as people of other religions do, or be repetitious with words. God, our heavenly Father, would have us be specific about our prayer.
- Jesus reiterates that the believer is not to pray repetitiously like the heathen.

NEXT, JESUS TEACHES US HOW TO PRAY

- Jesus says we should give honor to God and His Name. (Bless him and give him Thanks).
- We are to Pray for His Kingdom to Come, and for His will to be done, that there would be a heavenly or Godly presence here on earth.
- We are to pray for daily provision. (Trust in Jesus Christ as our personal Savior)
- We are to pray and ask for forgiveness for our sins, and for others who have wronged us.
- We are to pray and ask God to keep us from being tempted, and to deliver us from Satan and his power.

'A DYING FRIEND'

Recently I had lost a dear friend. She had Lukemia she only knew she had Lukemia for about 6 months. But the Lukemia didn't kill her she had two severe strokes that had taken her life. Before she died she had me to come over to her house and I held her hands and *whispered a prayer* just between us. After I said a prayer her face lightened up and she looked so much better. Her confidence became stronger and her face was brighter. I shared with her some of the things that God was showing me. She said I want to know more about Jesus. So, anything you have can you share with me? I was sharing with her through my text on the phone on some of the things God was showing me. I had just bought a Who Who's book a newer version of people of the Bible. I shared with her about Anna the Prophetess a woman mentioned in the Gospel of Luke. Anna was a widow and was up there in age. At her old age Anna was still fasting. The Bible paints her as a pious prophetess whose advanced age and honorable behavior usher in the new covenant. Then I mention to her how *angels* come and take you at the time of death. Yes, the Bible indicates that when we die we will not be alone, but angel(s) will accompany us on our journey to heaven. Read Luke 16:19-31; Hebrews 1:14; and Psalm 91:11. Tears started streaming down her face as I held her hands and she was lying on her back on the couch with not much energy. I wiped her tears with my fingers and kept on talking to her as if I didn't see the tears.

I knew I had to let her know about when our purpose in life is over. God helped me prepare her for her destiny to heaven. She was a delicate rose. I lost my dear friend May 03rd 2020. She was ready.

I was not intimidated to offer *whispers of prayer* for the dying death of my friend. Can you do it? The very fear we have and the grief we feel is also in the heart and mind of the one who is facing death. I had embraced the opportunity and shared with her. Jesus said in the Sermon on the Mount in Matthew 5:4 (NIV), "Blessed are those who mourn for they will be comforted." As we mourn with someone who is dying or with someone who's experiencing the death of someone close to them -- we need to give them comfort, and uplift them. To be a blessing to someone dear, gave me great comfort. I saw a lady struggling in her spirit to live. Fighting a fight that seemed as a losing battle; the dying will take any kind of quality of life that is offered them. She was grasping to live. Death comes when the struggle to cling to the flesh gives way. She accepted the journey that her spirit needed to take. Jesus knows that journey. He went through it. He conquered it for us. John 11:25 (NIV). ...one who believes in me will live, even though they die. Jesus alone is the judge of who inherits eternal life. So leave it in His loving, righteous, gracious, and worthy hands. I offered her Hope and Good News as she was dying away. The Good News is that death is now swallowed up in victory I Corinthians 15:54-57 (NKJV). For the believer, death is the gateway into the promise of eternal life as we shed our earthly bodies to enter into the presence of God I Corinthians 15:50-53 (KJV).

SHOULD I PURSUE?

"Should I pursue these raiders? Will I overtake them?" The LORD replied to him, "Pursue them, for you will certainly overtake them and rescue the people." I Samuel 30:8 (HCSB).

"So then let us *pursue* the things which make for peace and the building up of one another." Especially at time of death.

Fortitude *To strengthen your will*

"Let all that you do be done in love." I Corinthians 16:14 (ESV).

For perfect love, which comes from Christ, casts out all fear. That's what gives us power to move forward, propelled with His strength, surrounded in peace, eyes on the One who gives us breath each day. All that we do. All that we say. All that we stand for. Let's do it with love.

Problems are not stop signs, they are guidelines to our circumstances. God gives us Godly instincts.

'CLOSE TO GOD'

I have come to the conclusion that my close relationship with the Lord, humility, repentance, and living in alignment and obedience to the Word of God is the whole definition of spiritual warfare. I had to make the decision to trust & believe Him to be at peace. One battle is struggling with Patrick's legs with two broken knees one is fixed and the other is not fixed. A twisted foot that didn't heal right. Trying to keep balance with his heart after his heart attack. Diabetes watching what he eats… God has performed one miracle after another without us arranging things. If I fear & don't use a soft word to turn away wrath I'm disobeying God's Word. If I stay close to Him & His Word He goes before me to prepare me for the next issue. In Jesus' name is not a phrase to cast out demons. I live, work, play, & exist in the name of Jesus so I serve Him…not the news, church, family, job, or pastor…in spite of what I feel or see. The Bible has daily directions to fight our battles by renewing our mind, being conformed to His image, prayer in faith, discernment, knowledge, wisdom, discipline, and obedience… by the whispering of prayer *to the almighty. If a matter is important to you Take it to God.*

PRAYER

Father, in the Name of Jesus, I thank You that You desire to spend time with me, and You have even called me Your friend. God, Your Word says if I draw near to You, You will draw near to me—and I want to be near to You. So, right now, in the Name of Jesus, I draw near to You. Help me never to compromise the time I need to spend with you. In Christ Jesus amen.

'STORY OF HARDSHIPS'

Have you ever had a big situation in your life where you just couldn't process why God would allow this to happen? I have been there a few times... How about making choices that we think is right but, it goes the wrong way 'one after another'. I love the words in the bible Philippians 4:12-13 (NIV) "... *secret of being content in any and every situation, whether well fed or hungry, whether living in plenty or in want. I can do all this through him who gives me strength.*" We bought a house from a contractor in Dawsonville, Georgia a new little house. We lived there I think for about five years. During our time there we came across many obstacles. My daughter was fighting with awry girls that wouldn't leave her alone. She couldn't concentrate on her studies because of all the fighting. In the alternative school the children were sleeping in class. I went to court and the judge said, to me keeping her out of school I could send you to jail. He had mentioned about home schooling her. Home schooling was the best choice for her she finally was learning. Patrick was a rep and had been working for National Hardware. National Hardware sold out to another company and every rep was let go of their positions and left him jobless. During this time we were on Hwy 400 at a standstill turning off of the hwy and a car came around 80-100 mph hit us from behind and didn't notice we had stopped or we were even there? We climbed ourselves out of the vehicle and it rattled us severely our bodies were shaking. Both of us being tearful we looked at each other and were thankful we were alive. I had saved up some money to go in business to begin an Antique thrift shop. That was the plan. To my surprise the person opened up a shop without me? Things were happening one thing after another. We were trying to survive. We were having a garage sell after garage sell to exist. The money I saved for the Antique thrift shop I spent to pay on our mortgage. I went to a pawn shop in Dahlonega, GA and pawned my vehicle to get more money to pay our mortgage. After paying this man back for so many weeks I went in to make my payment and he said, "You have paid enough consider you are paid in full." Yes, "I said Thank You!" I had to file bankruptcy. The bank foreclosed on us after missing one payment they gave us notice we had to move in forty five days. I had no money not knowing what we were going to do. Patrick's (single) friend said we could live in one of his bedrooms but, my daughter could not come. I did not know exactly why but I think it had to do with his relationship at the time not wanting a single pretty girl living in the house. My daughter went to live with my sister. It was so difficult for me. A time of desperation and sadness.

It reminds of the song *'In Times Like These You Need A Savior'*.

During that time we practiced our whispers of prayer at dinner time. But in reality we didn't pray a lot otherwise. We didn't do drugs we didn't drink we were just living a normal life of contentment. God is always in our heart His seed is rooted deeply within. Prayer is a very simple thing, but many of us fail to receive its benefits because we don't pray. When we don't pray we lose a lot of the benefits that can only be received through a growing and intimate relationship with God. All of the great men and women of God in the Bible prayed. Many of them prayed all the day. Many of them prayed in times of trouble, even in times of great joy and happiness. If all of these men and women we honor as Christians prayed, what makes us think we can just work our way to greatness without praying?

We don't receive because we don't ask. Jesus said that those who ask receive, and those who seek find, and those who knock will have the door opened for them. God, of course, loves to bless His people even with surprises. But He wants us to open our hearts to Him and bond with Him in whispering prayer. And when we whisper a prayer to Him and get close to Him, we'll know His character and grow dependent on Him, which He likes and handsomely rewards.

Charles Spurgeon was said never to have prayed more than five minutes at a time, but he never went more than five minutes without praying. He often mentioned that the secret of his success was prayer, and he cited the many church members who prayed regularly in the basement during the services and on other significant occasions. He stated, to pray is to enter the treasure house of God and to gather riches out of an inexhaustible storehouse.

When we put God first in our life as God's Will this should give us confidence and faith that our prayers have been heard. By doing these things such as; putting God first, lean upon him, do what is good and right...God will order our steps and not allow us to be cast down and even if we make a mistake he will carry us and hold us up with his right hand, and this takes away all of our doubts. Telling the Father we love Him He will direct our will according to His promise and all doubt in our heart should be removed because He will order our steps to His plan and hears our plea and **God will protect us, guide us, uphold us, deliver us,** and we do not have to worry.

YOU'RE BEAUTIFUL

You are treasured, you are sacred, you
are His. You're beautiful.

I am praying that you have the heart to fight.

The heart transforms our lives, knowing that we are fighting for what we love. **God's *purpose* is behind our problems.**

When we live a sinful life, we then separate ourselves from God and because of sin our perspective and our approach to life's problems become ungodly....

Life is a series of problem-solving opportunities. The problems we face will either defeat us or develop us - depending on how we respond to them. God uses *problems* to DIRECT, INSPECT, CORRECT, PERFECT, and PROTECT us - Sometimes God must light a fire under us to get us moving. Problems often point us in a new direction and motivate us to change. "Sometimes it takes a painful situation to make us change our ways."

...discipline purifies the heart.

But your iniquities have separated you from your God; your sins have hidden his face from you, so that he will not hear. Isaiah 59:2 (NIV).

THRONE ROOM OF GOD

Sometimes we wonder are my *whispering prayers* reaching to the throne room of God? We must confess our sin and ask *forgiveness* before we can ask anything of God our sin *separates* us from the Living God.

God is at work in our life - even when we do not recognize it or understand it. But it's much easier and profitable when we cooperate with Him!

[People who have overcome abuse, or a tragedy any type of problems are more effectively able to comfort, empathize and counsel a person who is going through similar circumstances.]

GOD WANTS TO BUILD OUR CHARACTER

God is more interested in developing our character and becoming mature in Christ, so that we can cope with anything that life may throw at us. When we face circumstances, it might be that God wants to teach us specific values and virtues through our problems such as patience, perseverance, love, faith and the like. God can use *problems* to change our perspective about life and about Him. As for me I have had my share and I thank God for this *transformation*. With my husband Patrick his heart attack gave life near-death experience have been known to radically and positively change his outlook on life.

We may not understand the purpose of our challenges at the present, but they will make sense in the future when we have arrived at the place that God wants us to be in life. I didn't know that my freelance work at a manufacturing publishing company would help me today on what I am doing spiritually. I gave this work up in 1995 and God had taken my past skills to utilize for today.

It is important to understand that challenges and problems are not always present so that they may destroy us. We may step out of God's Will. In certain situations, God may use our problems so that He may achieve His will. For every circumstance we face, God is faithful and He will provide a way for us to escape and be victorious.

Sometimes God deals with our hearts to do something... such as my daughter he could had dealt with her heart and told her not to get in the car. But, she refused to listen to His call and did her own thing and it had taken her life. She stepped out of the protection of God. Red flags are there for a reason... don't ignore them. They are God's way of *protecting* us from something we can't see.

To experience the presence of God at all times, in all places. As we read of His many promises and assurances to us in the Bible, we'll come to realize just how much <u>He</u> <u>loves</u> <u>us!</u>

To experience the presence of God at all times, in all places was surely my aunt Mauga May Robertson who is deceased. She had faith like Kathryn Kuhlman. She sat erect and proper. When we would visit my grandmother my aunt Mauga would come over to her house. When I was about nine or ten years old she came over to me by my side and start talking to me to get insight of what I was doing in life. I proceeded letting her know. She said, let's go pray about this in the bedroom with her mighty faith. We get to the bedroom and she proceeds to whisper prayer over me. When we were done she had a smile on her lighten up face bright and radiant. I could tell she was a true devoted character with the faith of God at a young age.

Jesus many times was alone or sought out some alone time to draw strength from His Father.

ESTHER

As I am writing this script of my memoir I want this script to reflect God He is to be honored. I am alone like Jesus and He gives me the strength and ambition to be writing this. I feel I have been an orphan all my life. Esther words were "If I perish, I perish" Esther 4:16 (NIV): I can relate to this. Esther, a Hebrew orphan living in exile, teaches women to overcome such plights. Obeying her uncle Mordecai, young Esther auditioned at the palace and gained the king's favor, becoming a prestigious but powerless queen. Keeping her Hebrew heritage a secret, soon she learned that her race was to be exterminated by the king's orders. She promised Mordecai to petition the king, uttering the immortal words, "If I perish, I perish." What courage she had. Esther approached the king, which would cost her her life, if he refused her, and was granted his presence at a luncheon. With political savvy that belied her humble beginnings, she invited him again the next day, and there announced that she was a Hebrew and asked for the lives of her people. The book of Esther makes no mention of God, yet we see Him move powerfully through her to save the entire Jewish race. When we act in integrity before God, without manipulating, flirting, or relying on ourselves, God will make away for us. The Bible makes it clear that Esther was placed in her influential position for such a time as this—God's purpose was accomplished through Esther in the perilous time in which she lived.

When faced with sex discrimination, backbiters, intimidation, sorrowful attitudes or situations requiring great strength we must remember we have the mind of Christ and the power of God to overcome every obstacle. God within us is the VICTOR! We have a powerful God living with and in us. God is concerned with all of our needs.

GOD GIVES VICTORY TO THOSE WHO ARE IN HIS WILL

"The king's [decision maker's] heart is in the hand of the Lord. Psalm 146:7-9 (NIV) He upholds the cause of the oppressed and gives food to the hungry. Psalm 75:7 (KJV) But God is the judge: he putteth down one, and setteth up another.

GOD DOES THE CHOSING...

"No one can come to me unless the Father who sent me draws them, and I will raise them up at the last day." JOHN 6:44 (NIV).

God chose the one's who messed up Big Time. He chose the broken. He chose the one's who were looked down upon. He chose them IN SPITE of themselves... and He can use us too... like He is using me.

I want to encourage you to surrender your story to God. Give your life and your past and your todays and your tomorrows to Him. *Whisper a simple prayer* sincerely from your heart...

SAY THESE WORDS...

"God, I'm yours. I'm sorry about the mistakes of my life and those moments I chose me over You, but today I turn to You and ask for your forgiveness. Use my story for Your glory and help me rely on You completely each and every day." Thank You Lord. In your name I pray. Amen.

It is a trustworthy statement, deserving full acceptance, that Christ Jesus came into the world to save sinners, among whom I am foremost of all. Yet for this reason I found mercy, so that in me as the foremost, Jesus Christ might demonstrate His perfect patience as an example for those who would believe in Him for eternal life. I Timothy 1:15-16 (NIV).

We have left undone those things which we ought to have done; And we have done those things which we ought not to have done.

These two sentences diagnose the truth about our condition.

J. C. Ryle, the famous evangelical Anglican bishop of the late 1800s. In his book called Holiness, he wrote about how all the saints fall short of perfection:

The holiest actions of the holiest saint that ever lived are all more or less full of defects and imperfections. They are either wrong in their motive or defective in their performance, and in themselves are nothing more than splendid sins, deserving God's wrath and condemnation.

This is a much-needed word for a generation of Christians with an inflated sense of self-importance. Apart from God's grace, even our best efforts are nothing more than *splendid sins*. Our best efforts fall well over into the *splendid sins* category.

Our only hope of heaven is to run to the cross and lay hold of Jesus Christ. And we won't even do that unless God helps us to do it, and even then he must give us the strength to hang on and to keep believing.

> **Apart from God's grace, even our best efforts are nothing more than *splendid sins*.**

Jesus Christ has set us right with God, and now our whisper *prayers* can be powerful and effective, even like the prayers of Elijah.

One of the most important factors that shape our relationship with God is effective whispers of prayer. A successful *whispering prayer* life takes time, depth, commitment, knowledge of God and His word, self-awareness, and a strong belief in the love of God and His commitment to honor His word. Consistently answered prayer does not come easily. It is an art to be learned and a science to be studied. It belongs to both the humble and the strong. Whispers of prayer is easy, yet it is very complex. Successful whispers of prayer, however, is the key to a successful Christian walk.

When we allow God to control our motives and goals, then our desires are aligned with Him. Psalm 73:26 (NIV) says, "My flesh and my heart may fail, **but** God is the strength of my heart and my portion forever."

When we are able to have motives that are eternally focused and aligned with God's Will, we begin to realize that shift from emptiness to God's fulfillment within us. We will see that God is on our side, and He is working within us to fulfill those goals.

THE POWER OF
WHISPERED PRAYER

Psalm 107:28-30 (NIV) reminds us, "Then they cried out to the LORD in their trouble, and he brought them out of their distress. He stilled the storm to a *whisper*; the waves of the sea were hushed. They were glad when it grew calm, and he guided them to their desired haven." There is Power in the Whispers of Prayer!

I was totally inspired when I read about Jesus *whispering* to hush the seas.

The Power of whispers of prayer should never be underestimated because it draws on the glory and might of the <u>infinitely powerful God of the universe</u>!

"All the peoples of the earth are regarded as nothing. He does as He pleases with the powers of heaven and the peoples of the earth... Daniel 4:35 (NIV).

Therefore, since we have a great high priest who has ascended into heaven, Jesus the Son of God, let us hold firmly to the faith we profess. Hebrews 4:14 (NIV).

Let us then approach God's throne of grace with confidence, so that we may receive mercy and find grace to help us in our time of need.

JESUS WEPT FOR HIS FRIENDS

G od's Love - John 15:13 (NIV) ... "Greater love has no one than this, that HE LAY DOWN HIS LIFE FOR HIS FRIENDS".

Jesus Christ, is God's unique and eternal Son. He is the Alpha and Omega the Great I AM, the Mighty God by whom all things were created and in whom all things consist. Jesus, who is the head of all things humbled Himself in such a way that the human mind couldn't even bear the thought of it. He came into this sin-cursed world and actively partook in our sufferings. Even as we are flesh and blood, He shared in the same.

He became a man and dwelt among us. He shared in the sufferings we brought upon ourselves through our rejection of His holy precepts. And as if that were not enough to convince us of His love and concern for us, Jesus, the immortal God and the Giver of Life, gave up His own life upon the cross in the greatest act of love the world has ever known! In doing so He took our sins away, effectively nailing them to the cross with Himself. Thus, He who knew no sin became sin for us and He who gave life to all, tasted death for those condemned to it. See Hebrews 2:9 (NLT); 2 Corinthians 5:21 (NASB).

This is God's love! "For God so loved the world that he gave his one and only Son, that whoever believes in him shall not perish but have eternal life." John 3:16 (KJV).

BLESSED ARE THEY

Blessed are they who understand
My faltering step and shaking hand.
Blessed are they who know my ears today
Must strain to catch the things they say.
Blessed are they who seem to know
My eyes are dim, my mind is slow.
Blessed are they with cheery smile
Who stop to chat for a little while…
by Esther Mary Walker

Whispers of prayer is personal and without boundaries. Being of the realm of miracles it defies description. Everything is possible with whispers of prayer.

We whispers of prayer that come to us spontaneously in the form of gratitude, humility, and joy; they may arise in the midst of desperation and sadness when our physical and mental stage is about to break to its depletion. We come to whispers of prayer when our energy, have been sapped.

…we turn our attention towards God.

It is within the stillness, the humility of the heart, that we remember a relationship that has always been. We realize we are a vessel through which God's Love pours into our hearts.

Whispers of Prayer is an attitude, a way of action capable of informing and transforming every aspect of our self. Humbly expanding our prayerful attitude, in gratitude and openness, reveals our existing at or from the beginning of time a relationship with Love, with God.

God gives us the freedom to choose and perceive and free will allows us to select our concept of God. We select our perception, our attitude, our thoughts, and beliefs. As we become increasingly willing to trust and have faith in God, we come to experience a caring God offering an abundance of unconditional love, compassion, tolerance, patience, serenity, and peace. As we accept the Truth of God's love for us, we gain the capacity to set aside our old ideas and open to a new experience. By letting go of the past, within the present, we open to a personal relationship with God.

God wants us to be able to talk with Him with the same amount of frequency and with the same amount intensity as we would with our best friend. Except with God, He wants to become our Best Friend, over and above any of other best friends we may have in this Life.

God becomes number one in our life. He will not settle for number two position next to our family and friends. The Bible tells us that God the Father has a 'consuming type of fire' love for all of us, and He is very possessive and jealous over every single one of us with this kind of intense and passionate love. See Hebrews 12:29 (NIV) "God is a consuming fire."

With the above revelation telling us that we are free to boldly approach God's Throne and not to be afraid to state our cases and contentions before Him, and not to be afraid to try and reason with Him over certain issues and topics in our lives – what this now does is open up a whole new Realm of possibilities in our whispering prayer life with God the Father if we were never aware of this possibility before.

Once we have decided that we have a certain whispering prayer request that we would like to present before God the Father – the first thing we should decide is how strong we need to go in stating our case before Him. If our whispering prayer request is something very simple, we do not need to get all worked up and give God many reasons as to why we would like Him to grant our whispering prayer request. Just ask God once or twice and then have faith that He will answer the whispering prayer request as we walk in obedience.

However, where this principle will really come into play is when we have a request that is on the more medium to heavier side. A perfect example of something on the heavier side is when we may have whispers of prayer for someone who may be dying of Cancer as my other story my dying friend. This principle will really come into play on this type of emergency situation.

What we do in this type of case, is that before we start shooting 'Healing' and battle verses through and start asking God to Heal the one we are whispering prayer for – stop and form out our case as to why we would like God to heal this person. Stop and analyze the person's life that we are praying healing and extending this person's life.

When my friend Roy told me of his cancer he was a good Christian man. My reply to him was when God is finished with our purpose in life he will take us. I mentioned to him about David in the Bible.

"Now when David had served God's purpose in his own generation, he fell asleep; he was buried with his ancestors and his body decayed. Acts 13:36 (NIV).

God really does care for us and he cares for the person in whom we are praying for, and that He really does want to have a personal, two-way dialogue and conversation with us. We will learn that we can fully Trust Him and that He will always treat us Fairly, Honestly, and Justly.

IF GOD IS NO RESPECTER OF ANY PERSONS – then God will be giving us the same amount of time, care, and attention that He would be willing to give to anyone else – and this will also be including our own whispers of prayer with Him. We have just as much of a chance to get some of our own personal prayers answered with Him as anyone else.

"Trust in the LORD with all your heart and lean not on your own understanding",... Proverbs 3:5-6 (NIV). Say to the Father you said, if we Trust in you – you will direct our steps and we are relying on your deliverance in this whispers of prayer. This is what I did to get my deliverance in the story up above called 'Trust'. God delivered!

If God did it for Moses with the way Moses so passionately pleaded his case before Him with the rebellious children of Israel – then God can also do the same thing for us since the Bible tells us that He is no respecter of persons! See Romans 2:11 (KJV).

PRAYER

Our Loving Father, Thank You that the plans You have for us are prosperous. In Your loving way, you desire to be part of all we do simply for our good. Forgive us for the times we have gone about our duties leaving you out of the process entirely. Teach us how to approach what we do in faith and confidence, instead of in fear and doubt. Thank You that as we put you first in everything we do, our efforts will be blessed, to Your Glory. In Christ Jesus – amen.

—*Remember His words….*

In everything you do, put God first, and He will direct you and crown your efforts with success. Proverbs 3:6 (TLB).

Nothing is too small or insignificant to bring to Him in whispers of prayer.

It is necessary to put God first by asking Him to direct us.

By putting God first, we put the task(s) in His hands, and depend on His wisdom and power to complete it with success. It is our Loving Father who can give us creative ideas. Each time we approach a task, remember that there is our way of doing it, and there is God's way. If we humbly and prayerfully give it to Him, He becomes responsible for seeing that it succeeds. Do we sometimes face situations where we put in so much effort yet we do not get the desired output? Do we need to do something different? Then get our Loving Father intimately involved with what we do each and every time. God's plan is to prosper us and God will crown our efforts.

God will make us successful in everything we do according to His Will, What is God's Will> put Him first, give Him thanks for everything, lean not on our own understanding, do what is good. We can lay hold of that plan as we commit what we do to Him, and trust him to direct our efforts. Our efforts will be crowned with success.

My Journey with God... He pulled me out of despair & brought me into a life of 'Joy'! I wait patiently for the Lord.

I waited patiently for the Lord; and He inclined to me and heard my cry. He brought me up out of the pit of destruction, out of the miry clay, and He set my feet upon a rock making my footsteps firm. He put a new song in my mouth, a song of praise to our God …. Psalm 40 (NIV).

General Prayer Point – In our whispers of prayer always have confidence by putting God first he will answer our prayer. Pray that we will be strengthened, bonded with love and have mutual respect in our lives with each other. Pray specifically for everything in our lives and let God know of our heart for he already knows everything but, he wants to hear it from us.

If we go ahead with life on our own not talking to God, God is not obligated to direct our efforts, or to cause them to prosper. This is a recipe for frustration and failure.

David wrote: "Commit your way to the LORD; trust in him and he will do this." Psalm 37:5 (NIV) I want you to focus on the words, trust Him in this verse for a moment. No matter what task we may be facing now, God wants us to approach it in faith. He wants us to give it to Him, and believe with all our heart that He's going to help us with it. We can't approach an undertaking with fear and doubt and expect to achieve the same results that we would if we tackled it in faith. As the Bible says, And without faith it is impossible to please God, because anyone who comes to him must believe that he exists and that he rewards those who earnestly seek him. Hebrews 11:6 (NIV) Do we want our work to please God? Then get Him intimately involved with it each and every time.

"Bless all his skills, Lord, and be pleased with the work of his hands." [Whether we are using writing skills, ministry skills, cooking skills, or driving skills--We depend on the Lord to Bless them and to cause them to succeed for His glory]. God has a plan for our success in every endeavor we undertake, and we can lay hold of that plan as we commit our work to Him, and trust Him to direct our efforts. Large or small, we are committing all of our tasks to the Lord. Deuteronomy 33:11 (NIV).

DOES GOD ANSWER WHISPERING PRAYERS WHEN WE ARE IN DOUBT?

I am going to give you a scenario of what happened in the Bible when in doubt.

What happens when we have enough faith to approach God, to bring our concerns to Him, yet we still harbor some doubt in our hearts and minds? Will He hear us? Will He answer our prayers? What then? Well, the story in Acts 12:1-16 (NIV) describes that very scenario: Peter was in jail and "the church was earnestly praying" for him (v. 5). So, an angel came and released Peter from the jail. Peter went to the home where the church was praying for him. After Peter knocked at the door, a servant girl ran to the others to tell them Peter was there. "You're out of your mind," they told her. See Acts 12:15 (GNB).

Why did those praying for Peter doubt that it was him and assert that it must be his angel? Why were they astonished that he showed up at their door? Because there was at least some element of doubt in their minds and hearts that their prayers would be answered. Yet they were whispering prayer and God heard their prayers. And He answered them. We may say "God probably won't get involved in such a minor thing," or "This is just a shot in the dark. Doubt creeps in. But - I still whisper prayer. A bit of doubt when praying is it a good thing? Well, I certainly am not saying that it is. But I will say that it's better than having so little faith in God's love and power that we don't see any need to or benefit in praying at all. Still, God desires that our relationship with Him continue to grow such that our whispers of prayer are less and less clouded with any doubts. The more we whisper prayer, the more we will see God's power in answering our prayers, and the less we will doubt His ability and willingness to answer prayers in the future. - God is sufficient through all our emotions, feelings, doubts, fears and he understands each and every one of us and he will answer our whispers of prayer even when we are in doubt.

WHAT AN AWESOME FATHER WE HAVE!

All our works shall give thanks to You, O LORD, And Your godly ones shall bless You. They shall speak of the glory of Your kingdom And talk of Your power; To make known to the sons of men Your mighty acts And the glory of the majesty of Your kingdom. Your kingdom is an everlasting kingdom, And Your dominion *endures* throughout all generations. Psalm 145:10-13 (NASB).

One of the best prayers that we could ever whisper prayer is "God, Not My Will, but Your Will Be Done." If we will stay open to His direction, and follow our heart, God will protect us. See Luke 22:42 (NASB).

Some people say, "That God never answers my Prayers", someone may say, "He never does what I want."

Maybe God is answering our whispers of prayer; He's simply saying no. Or maybe He's saying it's not the right time. Or maybe He's saying, "I'm not going to remove that obstacle until you change your attitude and quit complaining about it." Make some simple adjustments, and we will see things begin to improve.

Relax and learn to Trust God. Know this: God is on our side. He is not trying to hold us back. No-one wants us to fulfill our destiny more than the almighty God. No-one wants us to see our dreams come to pass any more than God does. "He puts the dreams in our heart in the first place. Let Him lead us and guide us.

God knows what's best for us. When the job looked great at the time, and we didn't get the job and didn't know where God was taking us?

Too often, we're shortsighted. We can see only a little ways down the road, and even that we see through a glass dimly. God, though, can see the big picture. He knows when something is going to be a dead end. He knows when someone is going to be a distraction that will hinder us from our destiny.

Some of the things we may be frustrated about right now, in the long run we will look back and Thank God for not answering that whisper of prayer the way we wanted or for not opening up that door. We may not be able to see it right now, but that's what faith is all about. 'Why don't we Trust God?' Believe God has us in the palm of His hand and know that when it comes time for God to open a door, no man can keep it shut. No obstacle is too high. Our enemies may be powerful, but our God is All-Powerful. When God says it's time to promote us, we are going to be promoted. The Good News is that our promotion will not be one second late. Suddenly, God can turn any situation around. Suddenly. God can cause a door to open. .

ALL IT TAKES IS ONE TOUCH OF GOD'S FAVOR.

NO CHANCE OR LUCK OF THE GODLY

Jesus is teaching us that when a child of God dies, he/she is instantly delivered into the hands of a group of angels (and please notice he uses the plural for angel(s)), and they are in charge of delivering that person safely into the presence of God's rest. We must understand that chance is never a part of the language of life of the Godly. We are always under the sovereign care of God by the means of His angels, and so luck has no role to play in death either. We, dear child of God, are far too precious to go through this experience alone. God understands that our greatest fear is death. In His tender compassion, He has made every provision to comfort and protect us through the unknown by giving a multitude of angels charge to carry us to Him. See Luke 16:22 (NASB); Heb. 1:14 (NIV); and Ps. 91:11 (GNB).

No Reckless FATE, No Fickle CHANCE Rules Us

The steps of a good man are ordered by the Lord: and he delighteth in his way. Psalm 37:23 (KJV). All his course of life is graciously ordained, and in lovingkindness all is fixed, settled, and maintained. No reckless fate, no fickle chance rules in a believer; our every step is the subject of divine decree. He delighteth in his way. As parents are pleased with the tottering footsteps of their babies. All that concerns a saint is interesting to his heavenly Father. God loves to view the Holy strivings of a soul pressing forward to the skies. In the trials and the joys of the faithful, Jesus has fellowship with them, and delights to be their sympathizing companion.

For this God is our God forever and ever; he will be our Guide even to the end. Psalm 48:14 (NIV).

I will Instruct thee and Teach thee in the way which thou Shalt go: I will Guide thee with mine eye. Psalm 32:8 (NIV).

If God has a will for our lives, then it stands to reason that He wants to reveal it! Ephesians 2:10 (NIV).

[God is not playing "keep-a-way" with His Will.]

Psalm 148:1-4 (NASB)
Praise the LORD!
Praise the LORD from the heavens;
    Praise Him in the heights!
Praise Him, all His angels;
    Praise Him, all His hosts!
Praise Him, sun and moon;
    Praise Him, all stars of light!
Praise Him, highest heavens,
    And the waters that are above the heavens!

PIETY TO LOVE AND SERVE GOD

"Godliness with Contentment is Great Gain" I Timothy 6:6 (KJV).

Godliness and Contentment are indeed rare gems, but since they can only be found inseparably combined, they are the rarest of gem to be found in man. "Hearken, my beloved brethren, Hath not God Chosen the Poor of this World Rich in Faith, and Heirs of the Kingdom which He hath promised to them that Love Him?"James 2:5 (NIV). Unlike the covetous of the world, Christians are to be content with their lot in life—rich or poor, pleasant ways or a difficult road. Since they understand their physical circumstances to be both God's opportunity to mold them and reach the world. "To the weak became I as weak, that I might gain the Weak: I am made all things to all men, that I might by all means save some" I Corinthians 9:22 (KJV). Once it is fully realized that our physical circumstances ought to be treated only as secondary to our spiritual necessities, i.e., "Seek ye first the Kingdom of God, and His Righteousness; and all these things [food, clothing, shelter] shall be added unto you" Matthew 6:33 (KJV), then it becomes immediately possible to be truly content. "Let your conversation be without covetousness; and be content with such things as ye have: for He hath said, I will never leave thee, nor forsake thee" Hebrews 13:5 (NIV).

True Christian contentment is a satisfaction with God in His word, will, providences, promises, and prophecies. "In thy presence is fullness of joy; at thy right hand there are pleasures for evermore... a day in thy courts is better than a thousand. I had rather be a doorkeeper in the house of my God, than to dwell in the tents of wickedness" Psalm 16:11; 84:10 (NIV). The character of God is the great issue of Christian contentment. Are we truly satisfied with God? Do we really find our satisfaction in God's will for our lives? "From the end of the Earth will I cry unto thee, when my heart is overwhelmed: lead me to the Rock that is Higher than I" Psalm 61:2 (KJV). Can anyone actually show us a better way for our lives than what the LORD has already shown us?

KNOWLEDGE TO ENLIGHTEN YOUR MIND

Let's Pray:

Father, we thank You that Jesus Christ is our hope of glory. Because of Jesus, we have Hope. We may have turmoil in our life at this moment. Thank You for infusing your peace during our turmoil time. Thank You for increasing our Hope and Faith in Your divine presence in all circumstances. In Christ Jesus, amen.

I like the poem of Hope by Emily Dickinson

Hope Is The Thing With **Feathers** is one of the best known of Emily Dickinson's poems. An extended metaphor, it likens the concept of hope to a feathered bird that is permanently perched in the soul of every human. There it sings, never stopping in its quest to inspire.

Our life is in God's time. We often state these words, he gives us real lessons. I have many lessons to come, but I learned we worry during our circumstances but the Lord knows them all and He will deliver.

'LITTLE LESSON'

I recall when my daughter was a little girl she always wanted her mom to feel good. I was having it hard to provide for two little girls. All I did was go to work and rush to pick them up at the babysitter's and come home and feed my little ones. She went outside to play while I was making supper. Within in minutes she came running in to give me these beautiful flowers. I looked at the flowers and I knew she had taken them from someone's yard. I wanted to appreciate the flowers and the thought that she thought of me but I had to tell her that wasn't the right thing to do. Since, I had the flowers I did put them on the table in a vase. When she was eating supper she kept on staring at the flowers. I believe she felt good about the flowers even though I had to tell her it was wrong. I told her mommy loves the colors and they are very pretty but don't do that again. Heidi had always loved colors and coordination so I could understand her staring at the flowers.

My little girls I try to instill what was right in their life. One thing I instilled in their life from a very small child is not take God's name in vain. Little small things as being raised are rooted into their hearts. Just before my daughter died her friend came over to my house. She said, "Aleisha loved you very much and I had said <u>God</u> in a casual conversation." She said, "Aleisha corrected her and told her not to say that again." I then realized one small thing was important I did my job. The job now was being instilled into the legacy of God.

Train up a child in the way he should go: and when he is old, he will not depart from it. Proverbs 22:6 (KJV). The Bible verse that is quoted to suggest that if you do your job right as a parent they will believe. We must bring the child up God's way. "Bring a child up in his own way, and when he is old he will be stuck in his own way forever."

WISDOM TO VALUE THE THINGS OF GOD

When raising children the lessons don't need to be humongous but it is in the little lessons in life until they are grown up that they will remember God's words. I have many regrets raising my children it is a hard task of a single mom. I can sympathize when I see a parent having a hard time when the parent is teaching the child the right way. I have regrets but, I ask God to forgive my faults when it comes as a flashback in my mind.

The death of a loved one is traumatic, no matter the age especially when it is unexpectedly. It leaves a vacancy in our heart that nothing seemed to fill. Accepting someone as they are is a big issue today. Never criticize your children or the person you love. We mourn so deeply when the love one dies sometimes it affects the relationship with the Lord. I think of my mother who lost her son in Vietnam. I remember coming home from school and her door would be closed I could hear her praying over my brother Albert. But, after he died I do not remember her praying in her room anymore as she did. Love does not stop at death. Loving and missing the person will go on.

It is hard for me to think of our Father God, who was in heaven watching his son die on the cross. That he loved us even through the death of his Son - a Father who will never grow old, take ill, or decay or die. I think about when Jesus said: –

To the weak I became weak, to win the weak. I have become all things to all people so that by all possible means I might save some. Christ went through many things to be an example to many. I Corinthians 9 (NIV).

To this you were called, because Christ suffered for you, leaving you an example, that you should follow in his steps. I Peter 2:21(NIV).

When we cry and pray to the Lord during sadness he can relate to our hearts.

I think about this father being in jail. For over twenty five years he called daily. I could always hear words of encouragement being spoken to him. The father was about to come up for parole and possibly be released. During the twenty five years of anguish many tears daily flowed. It takes a strong person to encourage someone for twenty five years. Guiding a father to Jesus daily. But that is how our Heavenly Father is. God is with us to the end. Emotionally, mentally, spiritually was present continuously daily of encouragement. He was about to be released and fell and hit his head on the concrete. He was in the hospital for a short period then released. He was not healed. They released him back to jail before he was healed and he died. High hopes of being reunited, renewed with the father once again just diminished. Many stories of a (good dad). It was devastating news to be received and tearfully missed forever.

Feelings crumbled during sadness. The comforter came, the blessed Holy Spirit, rising up within us during the death of a loved one. Parting is such sweet sorrow. Having experienced the pain and sorrow of a love one's death.

Peter says...to whom shall we go? John 6:68 (NASB)

In the Bible Peter said Lord, to whom shall we go? You have the words of eternal life and we believe and know you are the Son of God. Peter was saying, Lord we seen too much, experienced things we never thought possible. We may still have some questions, but one thing we know is that you are indeed the Son of God and *where else can we go?*

Where can we go when death arrives at our door?

We start whispering prayer, "Oh, Lord help us during this time of sadness my heart is in shambles."

It reminds me when Lazarus died. Jesus loved Lazarus very much this is one of the times where Jesus wept over his friend.

GOD'S PERFECT TIMING

Scripture says in John 11:6 (NIV), "When Jesus heard that Lazarus was sick, He stayed where He was two more days. There is a reason for the delay....

Jesus had delayed his visit to raise Lazarus to show forth a miracle that we may not had seen. It also, shows delay of answering whispers of prayer at the present God is waiting for the right opportunity to answer our whispers of prayer for our best interest. God is planning something greater. We are thinking of a healing; He is thinking of a resurrection. We may be thinking how I can survive, but God is thinking how we can thrive. God will amaze us with His goodness in every area of our life! God has an appointed a time to fulfill the visions, dreams and desires in our heart. Just because it has taken a long time or because we've tried and failed doesn't mean it's not going to happen. God will even use our failures. Don't give up on those dreams! Don't be complacent about pursuing what God has placed in our heart. Our God is a faithful God. No matter how long it's been, no matter how impossible things look, if we'll stay faithful, our set time is coming. Remember, every dream that's in our heart, every promise that has taken root,

GOD PUT IT THERE!

Christ brought Lazarus back to life - Lazarus' life was not appointed for death. Many factors come to play at time of death, whether appointed or not – we need to make sure we are doing what is right in the sight of God and make sure if we are to die it is appointed by God – example: A man walking on wire and he knows if he falls his life is over so he goes ahead and tries it and falls and dies. His death was not appointed by God. "Jesus said, Take ye away the stone…And when he had spoken, he cried with a loud voice, LAZARUS COME FORTH" John 11:39-43 (NASB). Without this delay resurrection power would not have been experienced. Who among us today would not wanted to experience that resurrection power.

Desire to not experience such an occasion because we did not want to wait on the Lord to answer our prayers? Our whispers of prayer are answered by the Lord but in accordance with His divine will for our life and when he answers it is for the righteous man's betterment (so we do not have to worry or waver our whispers of prayer was heard and it will be answered).

The Lord will 'perfect' what concerns us. Psalm 138:8 (NKJV).

The Lord will perfect that which concerns me; Your mercy, O Lord, endures forever; Do not forsake the works of Your hands. We can know that God is mercifully working on our behalf and He will not forsake us.

"Only God can turn a mess into a message, a test into a testimony, a trial into a triumph, a victim into a victory!"

We become the Lord's best soldier through our circumstances. God teaches us through our circumstances and turns us around and utilizes us. He takes our past traits and uses them for the present and future for him.

God did his speaking through the writers of the Bible. Today He uses us. God speaks in whispers of prayer of thoughts that enter into our thinking. God whispers in the conversation called prayer. Have you ever had the thought pop into your head that you should visit someone right now to offer valuable help? Yes, I have.

I went to go visit my lost friend and when I arrived I had a flower to give her and to my surprise she was in the hospital. I gave her nine months of valuable help she needed so badly. This is the Holy Spirit at work in our thoughts and actions.

Remember the old picture of Jesus knocking at the door. All at once you see the picture of Jesus knocking at the door it initiates the conversation called prayer to talk to Him. God in his grace initiates the relationship of conversational prayer. We find ourselves responding.

My husband encounter happened when loading groceries into his car and discovering a gallon of milk that had not been bagged and thus wasn't paid for. What should I do the question pops up? It would be a big pain to go back inside and stand in line again. Besides, it was only a few dollars. The Spirit prevailed in that internal whispers contest in his head. Can anyone prove these are genuine encounters with the Spirit? No more than anyone can prove beyond doubt that God exists. He went back into the store and paid for his gallon of milk and the lady said Merry Christmas in the middle of July.

Be encouraged by the cloud of witnesses today who react to whispers from God and live daily Spirit-driven lives.

In the previous year my husband and I were laying on the bed and we were talking. We were finished talking and I rose up to go to do something. When I did I heard a whisper and it said his name. I looked down at him and I said did you hear that? He said yes. I said what did you hear? He said, someone whispered my name. I looked at him and said you are right. This can not be explained why did we hear his name being whispered? When mentioning this to others they think you are insane. I am thinking back in the 1990's when he had seven dreams one each night of seven days. The dreams were about a green door? Another time, he was sleeping and a whisper of his name woke him up. He walked outside following behind the hearing of the whisper. He went out the front door and sat down on the front steps. Angels came forth from the sky toward him singing he didn't see the angels but the sound was there. I don't know the reasoning behind any of these. But, it is factual facts. He went back to bed not understanding what had happened.

I think God wants our attention. He knows when we need him the most. ***The Holy Spirit shapes our life***. We need to guard our walk with the Lord and be close to Him at all times. Spiritual convictions guide our actions such as Patrick going back into the store to pay for the milk. Patrick attributes that most absolutely to the *whispering* of the Spirit to Him and he is so grateful!

DEAR GOD

Keep me going and lead me in the light and love of you. amen.

The Lord desires to speak to us each and every day and my prayer is that He speaks to your heart through these stories I hope this book gives you encouragement to begin your journey of seeking the Lord listening earnestly for the quiet whispers of prayer of His voice.

The Lord speaks to us in ways we can understand, if only we'll stop long enough to listen. I think He even uses humor, phrases, other people through conversation, signs on billboards, dreams, the word of God, ministry on the TV, etc. that He grabs our attention, to motivate us to show us what he wants us to do.

DIFFERENT DREAMS THAT I REMEMBER

One time I was having dreams one after another. So, I bought a good dream book. I come from a family who always have dreams. In the past I would dream about an old man for the longest. Then I dreamed many times of people chasing me and right when they were about to grab my feet I would start floating in the air and go over beautiful landscape until I woke up. Why I dreamed these dreams over and over I do not know. The old man dream last for many years? I felt secure around him and I liked being with him in my dreams. I had a long deep dream in 1987 my brother-in-law and I was wrestling on the grass and we looked up to the sky and saw items floating in the sky these are the items: a dark circle with a gold ring around it, a flat skeleton face, a stone club, a t-pee of burning fire? A huge square came down and stopped above our heads. Looking up in the object in was dark blue sky with tiny white stars I knew the object could read my thoughts. But I didn't know if this object was good or bad. I reached up to touch the object it wouldn't allow my hands to move into the object. A male audible deep voice came through the object when I reached and He said, "You haven't seen it all yet" and then the object disappeared. At that time a black horse came swiftly over the sky it had a rider but he was 'hazy' It kept going back and forth through the 't-pee of fire'. More people came to see and when they did everything disappeared. After waking up and drawing the items I folded the paper and stuck it away. There were more to this dream I am just mentioning parts of it.

Discernment is important in trying to analyze certain dreams, handling people in the right way, acknowledging mood swings, and recognizing colors etc.

Learning how to trust God through situations is important. Allowing ourselves to worry about life or stress about a situation will bring us down even more. One of God's many promises in the Bible tells us that God will supply all our needs, Phil 4:19 (KJV). But my God shall supply all your need according to his riches in glory by Christ Jesus. This, of course, is according to His will. What is His will one thing is put God first in everything.

Daily whispers of prayer is the most important thing we can do. I know life can get busy and sometimes causes us to say a whisper of prayer quickly – anytime saying a whisper of prayer is great.

God is the best thing for us. He knows what's best for us in every situation. Whispering prayer to God for wisdom should be our top priority. He can speak to us and give us words of encouragement anytime even in quick situations.

HIS FAITHFUL

However, there is absolutely nothing more important than communicating with God. When we whisper prayer daily we are equipping ourselves to face the challenges of the day.

Roll yourself upon the Lord early morning.

Roll your works upon the Lord [commit and trust them wholly to Him; He will cause your thoughts to become agreeable to His will, and] so shall your plans be established and succeed. The Lord has made everything [to accommodate itself and contribute] to its own end and His own purpose—even the wicked [are fitted for their role] for the day of calamity and evil. Proverbs 16:3 (AMPC).

WHISPERS OF PRAYER FOR LOVE

"God help us to 'love' as you have commanded us to 'love'. Help us, Father, to do right by those who have done us wrong."

A new commandment I give to you, that you love one another, even as I have loved you, that you also love one another. John 13:34 (NASB).

If we do not take the time to ask God to help us to love just as he loved us, it will not be long before we find ourselves walking in bitterness and not caring about the souls of man. Every day we should whisper a prayer for love so God can equip us to love one another.

DAILY PRAYER FOR PEACE OF MIND

Our peace of mind comes from *trusting God*. See John 14:27 (NLT) and Isaiah 26:3 (NLT). We *trust* that he is going to do just as he has said. Sometimes distractions come and take our eyes off of God. We *worry* about things like:

- What's going to happen if we lose everything?
- Our daughter moves out of state and we are afraid for her.
- Making the wrong decision.
- How are we going to survive without a job?
- How are we going to pay the bills?

Our minds become overwhelmed with worry and fear. Whatever peace we had, we lose. This is why we need a daily whispers of prayer for peace of mind. We need to pray and ask God to surround us with His peace. When the storms of life hit we need an anchor and that anchor is Jesus Christ. As a Christian we soon learn to cast all of our fears upon the Lord.

"Casting all your care upon Him, for He cares for you."
I Peter 5:7 (NKJV).

WHISPERS OF PRAYER FOR PROTECTION

Father, Thank You for putting Your hedge of protection and safety over us. God, hear our voice. Lord, listen to our prayer.

Thank you for walking with us with your Peace. Thank You for giving us Your angels charge over us to guard us in all our ways. We believe and trust you, please listen to our prayer. Thank You for keeping our hearts from fear but rather fill us to overflowing with Your peace that passes all understanding. You are indeed our refuge and strength. You are that ever present Help in time of trouble. Stay with us wherever we go. In Christ Jesus, amen.

BLESSINGS

Blessings, rewards and opportunities> When we commit to God He directs our paths in His will -- which is where our blessings, rewards, and opportunities are. Each time we approach a task, staying in His will by putting God first in everything. If we humbly and prayerfully give it to God, He becomes responsible for seeing that our task(s) succeeds. See Proverbs 16:3 (AMPC); James 4:7–8 (KJV).

David wrote: "Commit everything you do to the Lord. Trust Him to help you do it and He will."

Where can I go from your Spirit? Where can I flee from your presence? If I go up to the heavens, you are there; if I make my bed in the depths, you are there... Psalm 139:7-16 (NIV).

Matthew Henry's Concise Commentary

We cannot see God, but he can see us. The Psalmist did not desire to go from the Lord. Whither can I go? In the most Distant Corners of the World, in Heaven, or in Hell, I cannot go out of thy Reach. No veil can hide us from God; not the thickest darkness. No disguise can save any person or action from being seen in the true light by him. Secret haunts of sin are as open before God as the most open villanies. On the other hand, the 'believer' cannot be 'removed' from the 'supporting, comforting presence of his almighty friend'. Should the persecutor take his life, his soul will the sooner ascend to heaven. The grave cannot separate his body from the love of his saviour, who will raise it a glorious body. No outward circumstances can separate him from his Lord. While in the path of duty, he may be happy in any situation, by the exercise of faith, hope, and prayer. (NOTE: Remember when you accept 'salvation' you are given the gifts of faith, hope, and liberty (freedom)).

'SALVATION'

I recall when I was studying that I found out my salvation is irrevocable. Many claim to have salvation but they act like they lose their salvation and ask for it again and again. Salvation is a gift that God gives us.

for God's gifts and his call are irrevocable. Romans 11:29 (NIV).

Salvation is a Gift - If, we fall short or sin we need to ask forgiveness because if we don't there will be a gap of communication between us and the Father. Either we are for the Lord and allow him to order our steps and paths because praising God, giving Him thanks, etc is in the Will of God and we are blessed! Remember when we are walking in the will of God we are blessed, and his favor is upon us, and if we made a bad decision God will uphold us because we are righteous, and He will not allow us to be utterly cast down, and will reach out with His right hand and hold us up.

If we do not ask forgiveness for our sin (iniquity/sin) separates our communication with the Father. By, this we are whispering Amiss prayer where our prayers do not get answered. Amiss prayer is harboring sin within our hearts.

Ye ask, and receive not, because ye ask amiss, that ye may consume it upon your lusts. You ask and don't receive because you ask with wrong motives, so that you may spend it on your pleasures. James 4:3 (KJV).

"If I regard iniquity in my heart, the Lord will not hear but certainly God has heard me; He has attended to the voice of my prayer." Psalm 66:18-19 (NKJV).

I was so thrilled to know this. This was new to me and I felt like a heavy weight was lifted. Thinking of my husband's father worrying about his soul, and others who had accepted salvation and feeling they are lost. God don't play keep away *give and take*. The first promise to fully embrace is your righteousness in Christ. You are not a sinner. You are righteous through the blood of Jesus. All sins, past, present, and future, are covered by the blood of the lamb. No matter what we've done, we are righteous today if we believe in the Son.

"The LORD is good to all; he has compassion on all he has made..... You open your hand and satisfy the needs of every living creature." Psalm 145:9;16 (NIV).

When impatiently people jump into a relationship or a business deal that they didn't feel good about, but they wanted it so badly. God is a gentleman. If we insist, He will back off and let us do things our way. Most of the time when we do that, we end up *settling for second best.*

Our thoughts may be especially enabled to be directed to the face of God in the quietness of the morning before the rush of the day; but, anytime that you in faith Draw Nigh to God... He will Draw Nigh to You James 4:8 (KJV).

"And the LORD shall guide thee continually, and satisfy thy soul in drought, and make fat thy bones: and thou shalt be like a watered garden, and like a spring of water, whose waters fail not" Isaiah 58:11 (KJV). This promise of contentment is given especially to those who have fulfilled the condition named in the preceding verse of its context. "And if thou draw out thy soul to the hungry, and satisfy the afflicted soul; then shall thy light rise in obscurity, and thy darkness be as the noonday" Isaiah 58:10 (KJV). Notice the Beautiful mixture of spiritual and physical blessing promised to those who live their lives in an unselfish state of giving.

KNOW YOUR WHISPERING PRAYER IS HEARD

"Silver and gold have I none; but Such as I have Give I Thee: In the Name of Jesus Christ of Nazareth Rise Up and Walk" Acts 3:6 (KJV). As much as we are concerned about our own physical well-being -- "no man ever yet hated his own flesh" Ephesians 5:29 (KJV) -- our greatest concern should be that our heart is in the right place, and that our greatest satisfaction would be in God. "He hath done all things well: He,maketh both the deaf to hear, and the dumb to speak" Mark 7:37 (KJV). With Whatever Strength we can muster, if we will unrelentingly cast ourselves upon the LORD, we will find our greatest satisfaction and only then will we be truly content. "Cast thy burden upon the LORD, and He shall sustain thee: He shall never suffer the righteous to be moved" Psalm 55:22 (KJV)> We must commit our ways and works to the Lord; let him do as seemeth him good, and let us be satisfied. To cast our burden upon God, is to rest upon His providence and promise. And if we do so, he will carry us in the arms of his power; and will strengthen our Spirits by his Spirit, so that we shall sustain our circumstance. God *will never suffer the righteous to be moved; to be so shaken by any troubles, as to quit their duty to God, or their comfort in him.* HE WILL NOT SUFFER THEM TO BE UTTERLY CAST DOWN. See Psalm 37:24 (NKJV). He, who bore the burden of our sorrows, desires us to leave to Him to bear the burden of our cares, that, as he knows what is best for us, he may provide it accordingly. ***Why do not we Trust Christ to govern the world which he redeemed?*** As we whisper prayer we should have the confidence that he hears and his ear is open, are we giving thanks to the Father, and putting him first in our decision making, and doing what is good and right if so, then the whispers of prayer is to know our prayer is heard.

There is **no** spiritual life in the soul till the heart is circumcised, or, in other words, regenerated and renewed; then it is quickened in faith in Christ with communion with him, and both open right unto, eternal life. The ability to love the Lord & keep His commandments. Deuteronomy 30:6,8 (NIV) says "The Lord your God will circumcise your heart… to Love the Lord with all your Heart…and to obey the voice of the Lord and do all His commandments." Notice that the Lord said that He would do it. God must perform the work, but we must allow Him to circumcise our heart. Co-operation on our part is required! Also see I Corinthians 7:19 (NASB), where Paul implies that *the true meaning of circumcision is to keep The commandments of God.* The commandments are our guideline.

Remember, if we have been kept in a Holy walk before God, then content ourself that the great God that sustains the Lilies of the Field will continually be our *Secret Spring Bubbling* up in our innermost soul, "LIKE A SPRING OF WATER, WHOSE WATERS FAIL NOT" Isaiah 58:11 (NKJV). ANOTHER PROMISE FOR OUR CONTENTMENT emphasizes the *Joy and Blessing* that we find simply from the Word of God that we already possess."Thy Words were found, and I did eat them; and Thy Word was unto me the Joy and Rejoicing of mine Heart: for I am called by Thy Name, O LORD God of Hosts" Jeremiah 15:16 (KJV). No Doubt, the Joyful Blessedness described by Jeremiah is the same as the Psalmist, and is a promised picture of contentment for all those *who presently meditate in the Law of the LORD.* "By obeying God's ten commandments and *honoring God's Will* then rest assure our whispers of prayers are being heard! It isn't hard to wake up and say "Blessed be the name of the Lord for all that is within me, Bless his Holy name, Bless the Lord and forget not his Benefits" Say these words Morning and Night and Bless the Lord! Give him Thanks for everything, and put him first in our life, Roll your works upon the Lord [commit and trust them wholly to Him; He will cause your thoughts to become agreeable to His will, and] so shall your plans be established and succeed. Do you want Success? This must be our goal to please God and allow him to direct our life, by Him directing our life we will

Succeed in ALL WE DO.

"The Blessing of the LORD, it maketh rich, and He addeth no sorrow with it". Proverbs 10:22 (KJV;NIV).

Yet **the** LORD longs to be gracious to you; therefore he will rise up to show **you** compassion. For the LORD is a God of justice. Blessed are all who wait for him! Isaiah 30:18 (NIV).

PEOPLE SAY I AM IN THE VALLEY?
My God is not a God of Valley's he is a God of High Favor

Valley's are for people who disobey God - In God there are no valley's if you are walking right you are favored - God will allow you to be favored among the Godly and ungodly alike - "No one can serve two masters. Either you will hate the one and love the other, or you will be devoted to the one and despise the other Matthew 6:24 (NIV). So, if you love God you will *obey* him and God will implant upon your heart - you are totally His - people use '*Satan*' as an excuse to be disobedient in their lives - the disobedience causes, valley's, hardships, a gap between you and God, you have to sever back your relationship by *asking forgiveness* for what God deals with you upon your heart - God says because he loves me I will answer him and because he calls upon my name I will answer him and give him my

— FULL SALVATION —

Salvation encompasses both the physical and spiritual dimensions of life, having relevance for the whole person – Our soul gets restored unto Christ - so in Christ there is *no valley'* God wants us to prosper he takes delight in our prosperity see Psalm 149:4 (NASB) - God is good all the time and he is in control of the bad and the good - But, there are specifications to walk in the Will of God to be blessed and if we are being blessed (there is no valley) - A lot of Christians are *wishy washy* and take it upon themselves they have to have a valley but in reality my God is not a God of valley's he is a God of high favor. **Because God is in control we can trust God in whatever circumstances we find ourselves.** See Matthew 5:45 (ESV).

The words "Yea, though I walk through the valley of the shadow of death"... See Psalm 23:4 (KJV). "The Hebrew word for "shadow of death" is **sal-ma-wet**, which means "darkness" or "dark shadows." We have terrible frightening and shadowed places in life's journey when we scarcely know what the next step is to take. It speaks of those times and places when the beauty and serenity of life is either threatened or shattered by crisis or tragedy. There is nothing calm or soothing about this scene, but it is the reality of living in this world we cause a lot of our turmoil by our own *disobedience*. We live in a fallen fragile world. Every good and perfect gift is from above, coming down from the Father of the heavenly lights, who does not change like shifting shadows. James 1:17 (NIV).

God gave Mercy through our disobedience. Ephesians 1:18,19 (ESV).

I ask that the eyes of our heart may be enlightened, so that we may know the hope of His calling, the riches of His glorious inheritance in the saints, and the surpassing greatness of His power to us who believe. He displayed this power in the working of His mighty strength,...THEREFORE GOD DOES NOT TURN AWAY OUR WHISPERS OF PRAYER, BECAUSE HE DOES NOT TURN AWAY HIS OWN MERCY but, if you have iniquity (sin) in your heart he will not hear - Ps 66 (NASB) If I regard wickedness in my heart, The Lord will not hear; But certainly God has heard; He has given heed to the voice of my prayer.... When we go to whisper prayer ask for the forgiveness of all our sins before approaching and asking God's favor do not harbor sin within our heart...

"O taste and see that the LORD is Good: Blessed is the man that Trusteth in Him" Psalm 34:8 (KJV).

I desire to be righteous with God I know if I do God's Will *my* whispers of prayer is powerful and effective and I know my *whispers of prayer* makes it through the Throne of God.

The **Israelites** were *surrounded* by a huge army and greatly outnumbered. They were so worried and stressed out. Just before they went to battle, they decided to pray. Notice God's answer. If you will be still and remain at rest, God will turn it to victory.

...for the battle is not yours, but God's

The power of prayer is proved from the history of Elijah. In prayer we must not look to the merit of man, but to the grace of God.

Our thoughts must be fixed, desires must be firm and with enthusiasm or passionate. GRACES exercised. This Instance of the Power of whispers of prayer, encourages every Christian to be earnest in whispers of prayer. God never says to any of the seed of Jacob, seek my face in vain. I didn't **say** to the **seed of Jacob**, '**Seek** me **in vain**.' I, Yahweh, speak righteousness Isaiah 45:19 (KJV). Where there may not be so much of a miracle in God's answering our whispers of prayer, yet there may be as much of grace. His free grace is not tired nor grown weary. Certainly divine mercy > is an ocean that is ever full and ever flowing. Hurry with your answer, God! I'm nearly at the end of my rope. Don't turn away; don't ignore me! That would be certain death. If you wake me each morning with the sound of your loving voice, I'll go to sleep each night trusting in you.

Point out the road I must travel Psalm 143:10 (MSG) "Teach me to do what pleases you, for you are my God."

May your kind presence lead me into a level land "We must be 'enlightened with the knowledge of God's Will'; and this is the first work of the Spirit - a good man does not ask the way in which is the most 'Pleasant Walking', but what is the 'Right Way'. Those who have the Lord for their God, have his Spirit for their Guide; they are led by the Spirit. (Note: next time you have to make a decision remember you are led by God's Spirit) God teaches us in three ways. **First, by his word. Secondly, he illuminates our minds by the Spirit. Thirdly, he Imprints it in our hearts and maketh us obedient to the same**; for the servant who knoweth the Will of his Master, and doeth it not, shall be beaten with many Stripes: **Luke 12:47 KJV** knowledge without obedience is lame, obedience without knowledge is blind; and we must never hope for acceptance if we offer the blind and the lame to God." The Fruit of the Spirit is in all Goodness and Righteousness and Truth." Ephesians 5:9 (KJV) 'The fruit of the light is in all goodness and righteousness and truth.'

David prays that God would be well pleased with him, and let him know that he was so. Read chapter Psalm 143 (KJV). He pleads the wretchedness of his case... But the might of distress and discouragement shall end in the morning the comfort received with praise. He whispers of prayer that he might be enlightened with the Knowledge of God's Will; and [**this is the First work of the Spirit'**]. Not only show me what Thy Will is, but Teach me how to do it. Those who have the Lord for their God, have His Spirit for their guide; they are led by the Spirit. He prays that he might be enlivened to do God's Will. But we should especially seek the destruction of our sins, our worst enemies, that we may be devotedly God's servants.

Being a teachable person is quite important to God. His Intent is to teach us so much! He is the leader of our teaching, not the other way around. Through prayer, fasting, and reading scripture, seek to get on God's page about things in our life.

In Heaven, what is Jesus Praying for?

"Therefore he is able to save completely those who come to God through him, because he always lives to intercede for them." Heb. 7:25 (NIV).

Jesus Christ is still acting as our mediator through the union of his divine and human nature. In other words, it's not as if his human nature fell off as he ascended into heaven. Part of the Essence of Jesus' priestly work IS THAT HE STILL HAS A HUMAN NATURE, along with his Divine. It may be glorified, but he is still like us and able to act on our behalf. We could easily conclude that his heavenly priestly prayers are not too different from his earthly priestly prayers (see Luke 22:31-43 (NIV); John 17 (ESV)). In a very real way, his prayers for us are Human. Jesus' heavenly prayers are no more metaphorical than his earthly ones were metaphorical Jesus died a real death, took on real wrath, and paid for real sins.

And THANKS BE TO GOD, OUR SINS ARE FORGIVEN. The apostle John writes in I John 2:1 (KJV), "But if anyone does sin, we have an advocate with the Father, Jesus Christ the Righteous." Though John is speaking to believers, HE IS NOT CLAIMING THAT WE NEED TO BE SAVED EVERY TIME WE SIN. HIS SACRIFICE IS ONCE AND FOR ALL TIME.

But if we do sin we have one, namely Jesus Christ, who, on the basis of his death, calls attention to his perfect righteousness in defense of sinning saints. Jesus warns Peter, "Simon, Simon, behold, Satan demanded to have you, that he might Sift you like Wheat, BUT I HAVE PRAYED FOR YOU THAT YOUR FAITH MAY NOT FAIL... Luke 22:31-32 (ESV).

The Lord bless you and keep you; the LORD make his face shine on you and be gracious to you; the LORD turn his face toward you and give you peace. Numbers 6:24-25 (NIV).

Whispers of Prayer develops our
Relationship with God
Why should we whisper prayer?

If we never speak to our spouse or never listen to anything our spouse might have to say our friendship relationship will quickly deteriorate. It is the same way with God. Whispers of Prayer — communicating with God—helps us grow closer and more intimately connected with God. Zechariah 13:9 (NIV) ... They will call on my name and I will answer them; I will say, they are my people, and they will say, the Lord is our God.

But if you stay joined to me and my words remain in you, you may ask any request you like, and it will be granted! John 15:7 (NLT).

"Watch and pray so that you will not fall into temptation. The spirit is willing, but the flesh is weak." Matthew 26:41 (NIV).

There is freedom waiting for us.

'GRATITUDE'

I am thinking this morning about Fanny Crosby who wrote 'Blessed Assurance. In her autobiography, Frances Jane Crosby wrote, "It seemed intended by the blessed Providence of God that I should be blind all my life, and I thank Him for the dispensation."

The doctor who destroyed her sight in her infancy never forgave himself, but there was no room in Fanny's heart for resentment. "If I could meet him now," she wrote, "I would say Thank you, thank you over and over again for making me blind."

Crosby accepted her blindness as a gift from God with a special purpose. "I could not have written thousands of hymns," she said, "if I had been hindered by the distractions of seeing all the interesting and beautiful objects that would have been presented to my notice."

For over a century, the church has reaped the benefits of one woman's thankful heart as we sing "To God Be the Glory," "Blessed Assurance," "All the Way My Savior Leads Me," and countless other songs that Fanny Crosby wrote in her lifetime.

Why did I think of Fanny? I was thinking about gratitude.

My husband was leaving the driveway this morning. He stopped at the end of the driveway and he said 'God asked, him did he pray this morning?' He said no, I didn't pray. So, he stayed in position and whispered prayer. After he whispered the prayer *gratitude* rose up in his heart.

I seem to think this is discernment the ability to decide and judge between truth and error, right and wrong.

Do not ask God to guide us if we are not willing to move our feet. Patrick was quickly moved by the Spirit speaking to him and he immediately moved.

The Lord instructed us to PRAY

Then Jesus told his disciples a parable to show them that "they should always pray and not give up". Luke 18:1 (NIV).

And pray in the spirit on all occasions with all kinds of prayers and requests.... Ephesians 6:18 (NIV).

WHAT IF I DON'T KNOW HOW TO PRAY? The Holy Spirit will help you in prayer when you don't know how to pray Romans 8:26-27 (NIV). ..he who searches our hearts knows the mind of the spirit, because the spirit intercedes for God's people in accordance with the will of God.

GOD PROMISES US PROTECTION

If you read any of my stories at the beginning of this script I was protected by God.

God's promises us protection and a long life. If we obey all his words and commands, we will enjoy a long life. We can go to God Most High **to *hide*.** We can go to God all-powerful for protection. I say to the Lord, "You are my place of safety, my fortress. My God, I trust in you." Psalm 91 (NIV).

God cannot lie, we can have absolute confidence in His promise of protection. Protective power – God is for us a refuge.

In hope of eternal life, which God, that cannot lie, promised before the world began. Titus 1:2 (KJV).

By comparing himself to a shepherd, Jehovah assures us of his heartfelt desire to protect us. Ezekiel 34:11-16 (KJV).

Jesus' arm will collect together the lambs; and in his bosom he will carry them. He shall feed his flock like a shepherd: he shall gather the lambs with his arm, and carry them in his bosom, and shall gently lead those that are with young. Isaiah 40:11 (KJV). How does the little lamb come to be in the shepherd's bosom— cradle in his arms? The lamb might approach the shepherd, even nudge his leg. However, it is the shepherd who must bend over, pick up the lamb, and gently place it in the security of his bosom. What a tender picture of the willingness of our Great Shepherd to shield and protect us!

God's promise of protection is conditional — it is realized only by those who draw close to him. Proverbs 18:10 (ASV) states: The name of Jehovah is a strong tower; the righteous runneth into it, and is safe.

Jehovah has done more than just promise protection. In Bible times, he demonstrated in miraculous ways he is able to protect his people. During Israel's history, Jehovah's mighty hand often kept powerful enemies at bay. Exodus 7:4 (NIV) However, Jehovah also used his protective power in behalf of individuals.

When three young Hebrews—Shadrach, Meshach, and Abednego—refused to bow down to King Nebuchadnezzar's image of gold, the furious king threatened to throw them into a superheated furnace. "Who is that god that can rescue you out of my hands?" taunted Nebuchadnezzar, the most powerful monarch on earth. The three young men had complete confidence in the power of their God to protect them, but they did not presume that he would do so. Hence, they answered: "this is true, that the God whom we serve can save us." Daniel 3:17 (AMP). Indeed, that fiery furnace, even when heated seven times hotter than normal, presented no challenge to their all-powerful God. He did protect them, and the king was forced to acknowledge: "There does not exist another god that is able to deliver like this one."— see Daniel chapter three.

Comical humor in the bible

I LOVE IT WHEN ELIJAH SAID IN I KINGS MAYBE YOUR GOD IS ON THE TOILET?
I Kings 18:27 NIRV

At noon Elijah began to tease them. "Shout louder!" he said. "I'm sure Baal is a god! Perhaps he has too much to think about. Or maybe he has gone to the toilet. Or perhaps he's away on a trip. Maybe he's sleeping. You might have to wake him up."

… Elijah said to them, "Seize the prophets of Baal. Do not let one of them escape." And they seized them. And Elijah brought them down to the Wadi Kishon, and killed them there. Then Elijah told the spectators to slaughter the 450 prophets of Baal.

How about the comical of Peter when he told Jesus in John - "No," said Peter, "you shall never wash my feet." **Jesus** answered, "Unless **I wash** you, **you have no part** with **me**." "**Then**, LORD," Simon Peter replied, "not just my *feet* but my *hands* and my *head* as well!" James 13:8-10 (NIV).

There has never been a time, my friend,
When a broken spirit did not mend…

Have you ever had a *broken heart* in a relationship and
you believed in the words of the person?

I have and it tore me to pieces. I thought I didn't love the person and eventually I was going to move on. I trusted in his words not thinking I was being deceived. The only bad thing is I believed in the words of the person on what they were saying to me. Even though I kept a piece of my heart to myself. One day I came home and a table with roses left on the table with a meal. This melted my heart. I was working hard day and evening. My evening job was a part-time job to get through Christmas. I had two little girls depending on me for a happy Christmas. At times our instinct kicks in and we know something is wrong. I realized I did love the persons virtues but not his ways. I found emptiness creeping in and differences that didn't match. The relationship didn't work out. My heart was broken but, God heals broken hearts. I met another man months later that helped heal my broken heart. In a new relationship we both trust and believe in the Lord with all our hearts. This broken heart met another broken heart which is my current husband. He had his own story he burned my ears off telling me about his broken heart and it helped me to heal my broken heart. Betrayal of words hurts. Our God knows just what He is doing.

PRAYER FOR STRENGTH AND GUIDANCE

(a prayer for those going through a difficult time)

O Lord, I give You my worries and concerns and I ask for Your guidance. You see it all, the outer circumstances, the inner turmoil. I know that you understand my life, that sometimes my heart weighs heavy with trouble. Right now I lay all these things before You. May I be alert to your spirit's guiding as I journey onwards with You. I love you Father. In Christ Jesus amen.

LET GOD'S PROMISES SHINE ON OUR PROBLEMS

Nor are the yes of the man are ever satisfied Proverbs 27:20 (NASB). Instead, may we be as a Solomon, when he contented himself in seeking after the Living God, and concerned himself only with acquiring the *wisdom, discernment, and judgment* to obey Jehovah in shepherding his Kingdom in fulfillment of his kingly duties. …I have given thee a wise and an understanding heart; so that there was none like thee before thee, neither after thee shall any arise like unto thee. And I have also given thee that which thou hast not asked, both riches, and honour: so that there shall not be any among the kings like unto thee all thy days" I Kings 3:11-13 (NIV).

God gave Solomon wealth for a reason. The reason was because, when God promised Solomon that He would grant any request,

Solomon asked for wisdom to rule the people. God was so pleased that Solomon didn't ask for wealth (among other things) that along with wisdom He also gave him wealth. Solomon, however, didn't use His divinely-given wisdom as God intended, and he consequently became the most foolish man who ever lived.

How did Solomon ask God through whispers of prayer.

What are we to learn from the Prayer of Solomon? No matter who we are: rulers or common people, rich or poor, we must all come before God in humility.

The prayer of Solomon shows that he prayed to God asking Him to bring to pass the promises He had given to David.

God responded by saying, And the Lord said unto him, I have heard thy prayer and thy supplication, that thou hast made before me: I have hallowed this house, which thou hast built, to put my name there for ever; and mine eyes and mine heart shall be there perpetually. And if thou wilt walk before me, as David thy father walked, in integrity of heart, and in uprightness, to do according to all that I have commanded thee, and wilt keep my statutes and my judgments: Then I will establish the throne of thy kingdom upon Israel for ever, as I promised to David thy father, saying, There shall not fail thee a man upon the throne of Israel. I Kings 9:3-5 (KJV).

Know therefore that the LORD your God is God, the faithful God who keeps covenant and steadfast love with those who love him and keep his commandments, to a 'thousand generations'. Exodus 20:6 (ESV).

Both hundred years and forty years are a generation in the Bible. However, the average of these two, seventy years, is on occasion also found in the Bible, see Psalm 90:10 (NIV). Our days may come to seventy years, or eighty, if our strength endures; yet the best of them are but trouble and sorrow, for they quickly pass, and we fly away. But seventy years is a generation according to the average age of a man at his death. (as with the example of Abraham).

40 + 100 = 140 years. 140 ÷ 2 = 70-years as a generation. Significantly, king David died at age seventy, and reigned forty years.

That is a mighty long time to be loved by God.

David's words I like – "I said, "Oh, that I had the wings of a dove! *I would fly away* and *be at rest*." Psalm 55:6 (KJV).

FLY AWAY

Fly away my dove,
Spread your wings and fly;
Take the beauty of your wings,
And learn how to fly…

"For poverty He has given me wealth, for sickness He has given me health, for death He has given me eternal life."

Just open our eyes and open our heart and feel our worries and care depart.

… Do not let those who wait for you be put to shame; let them be ashamed who are wantonly treacherous. Make me to know your ways, O LORD; teach me your paths. Lead me in your truth, and teach me, for you are … Psalm 25:1-3 (NRSV).

For he will command his angels concerning you to guard you in all your ways. Psalm 91:11 (NIV).

YOU RAISE ME UP

'HEZEKIAH'S'

Whispers of prayer

ezekiah's prayer was Certain… Because it was based on his personal faith and trust in God. Hezekiah prayed, "Now, O LORD our God, deliver us from his hand, so that all kingdoms on earth may know that you alone, O LORD, are God." Isaiah 37:20 (KJV). Hezekiah had a faith in God that allowed him to pray with confidence.

Hezekiah prayed to the LORD: "LORD, the God of Israel, enthroned between the cherubim, you alone are God over all the kingdoms of the earth. You have made heaven and earth. Give ear, LORD, and hear; open your eyes, LORD, and see; listen to the words Sennacherib has sent to ridicule the living God. "It is true, LORD, that the Assyrian kings have laid waste these nations and their lands. 2 Kings 19:15-19 (NIV). They have thrown their gods into the fire and destroyed them, for they were not gods but only wood and stone, fashioned by human hands. Now, LORD our God, deliver us from his hand, **so** that all the kingdoms of the earth may know that you alone, LORD, are God." 2 Kings 19 (NASB)

"For Sheol cannot thank You, Death cannot praise You; Those who go down to the pit cannot hope for Your faithfulness." The living, only the living, can thank You, as I do today; fathers will tell their children about Your faithfulness... Hezekiah had confidence, he believed in his God. Isaiah 38 (NASB).

God had sent prophet after prophet to His people, Israel, and yet at every turn of the road they seem *to be* rushing after other gods.

I'm not a great person like Daniel or Moses but I can relate to Esther, Ruth and I love Anna she was so old but yet still was fasting at an old age. How can I expect God to be interested in my whispers of prayer? The answered prayers of Gideon give us a graphic account of the interplay between the Angel of the Lord and Midian. Midian was not known as a mighty man of stature, but was just an ordinary person like you and me.

How great is our faith? The whisper prayers of Hannah teaches us of Hannah's great faith and her powerful prayer, helping us to learn the proper way to approach and view our troubles and our adversaries, and how to take them to God in prayer.

What do we do when we are in a tight pinch? I think of Jehoshaphat when he sent the praisers out and turned his thoughts into a prayer before the battle.

Do we find our-self calling out to God for help when troubles seems to overpower us, promising to be more faithful to Him, and then forgetting that promise to God when everything returns to normal?

I think how we make a vow to God in time of crisis. Then forget God altogether after God answers the whispers of prayer.

Though God advises us not to vow, we can still make vows if we so choose.

CHOOSE
TO SHINE

It is better **not to** make a **vow** than to make one and not fulfill it. Ecclesiastes 5:5 (NIV).

We can promise a —vow— to change our way of living or do some specific deed in return for a request we ask from God. Should we do this? Is this wise? Should we really count the cost before we allow this thinking to be placed into action?

'HANNAH'

Samuel I - narrates the story of Hannah, the wife of Elkanah. She was barren, but with every fiber of her being, she desired a child. Though Elkanah treated her with love and kindness, his other wife, Peninnah, who had children, became Hannah's adversary, provoking her until she was miserable. Wisely, Hannah had taken her situation and desire to God. She vowed that if He gave her a son, she would give him to God for His service. I Samuel 2:1-10 (NIV).

She was in bitterness of soul, and prayed to the LORD and wept in anguish. Then she made a vow and said, O LORD of hosts, if You will indeed look on the affliction of your maidservant and remember me, and not forget your maidservant, but will give your maidservant a male child, then I will give him to the LORD all the days of his life, and no razor shall come upon his head. I Samuel 1:10-11 (NKJV).

In verses 19-20, God hears Hannah and gives her desire to her:

And Elkanah knew Hannah his wife, and the LORD remembered her. So it came to pass in the process of time that Hannah conceived and bore a son, and called his name Samuel, saying, "Because I have asked for him from the LORD." I Samuel 1:20 (KJV).

It is important to devote our children to the Lord.

God had fulfilled His part of the agreement, and now it was Hannah's responsibility to keep her promise. She holds up her end of the bargain.

'JEPHTHAH'

J|ephthah made a vow. He vowed rashly, without counting the cost to himself or to others. He seems not to have considered what the payment might be. He desired victory so greatly that he gave little thought to his part of the bargain. It was, as if he were saying, "Just give me what I am asking for, and I'll worry about my end later." Jephthah's rashness and inconsideration cost him dearly.

THE RULES OF VOWING

What are the rules concerning the making of vows? This is so important to God that He devotes a whole chapter, Numbers 30, to this subject. Immediately, we need to note that this instruction comes from the Lord, the One who became Jesus Christ. These rules are not just judgments of Moses but direct commands of God.

Verse 2 emphasizes that a person must always keep his word. Whether he swears an oath or vows a vow, he is bound to fulfill all its terms…

It is better not to make a vow than to make one and not fulfill it. Ecclesiastes 5:5 (NIV).

'MANASSEH'

2 **Chronicles 33 (NIV)** give specific details of the sins of Manasseh which brought upon him the wrath of God. Even though God spoke to Manasseh and his people, they would not listen to His entreaties to change their ways. God then allowed the king of Assyria to overpower Manasseh, bringing him to Babylon; in the prayer of Manasseh during his captivity, he finally submitted himself to God, crying out to Him for help.

Because Manasseh humbled himself before God, he was again restored to his throne in Jerusalem. It is not uncommon for us to call out to God for help when troubles seem to overpower us, and then to forget our promises to God when everything returns to normal. This, however, is not the case with Manasseh. Verses 15 and 16 reveal to us the change of heart and life upon Manasseh when he humbled himself before God.

The answered prayer of Manasseh provides a wonderful lesson to us of the power of God in the life of each person who humbles himself before God. Are we too wicked to ask for *'salvation'* from God? No! Manasseh's conversion was not just a simplistic means to get out of trouble; it was a complete change of heart and life.

'ANNA'

It was just recently when I was studying for the Inspirational Words page on facebook that I ran into Anna the Prophetess a Jewish woman. I shared my findings with my friend who was eighty years old. We both enjoyed thinking of an elderly lady who was a hundred and five years old. Many Bibles and older commentaries state that she was eighty fours years old. She never left the temple but worshiped night and day, with fasting and praying. She appears in Luke 2:36-38 (KJV) during the presentation of Jesus at the Temple. Coming up to them at that very moment, she gave thanks to God and spoke about the child to all who were looking forward to the redemption of Jerusalem.

She was a widow of eighty four years plus.
She knows who Jesus is immediately and how significant he will be.

Anna waits. And waits.

... long, long years she has waited for the Holy One of God. You can find her in Luke 2:36, (ESV).

Anna holds Jesus in her arms.

The Jewish people have waited a long time for their Messiah.

Mary and **Joseph** are there at the Temple because they have brought their newborn son Jesus for the customary ceremony.

…a purification sacrifice had to be offered see Leviticus 12:2-8 (NIV).

Moreover, a first-born child, male or female, had to be redeemed and consecrated to God.

Anna is a holy woman concentrating all her remaining energy on communion with God.

The moment described in Luke's 2:36-38 (NIV) gospel, Anna steps forward into center stage. Overcome with sublime joy, she begins praising God for what she knows has happened.

The Greek word used by Luke suggests recognition, intuition. **She sees what others cannot.**

Her reaction is immediate and dramatic: she speaks in as loud a voice as she can muster, telling anyone near her about this extraordinary child.

Here, in front of their eyes, is the Being who will bring redemption to Israel.

Anna/Hannah means grace or favor. She is identified as the daughter of Phan'u-el

Phan'u-el means face of God. His name may be a play on words, since Anna was among the first to recognize the face of God when she saw the infant Jesus.

THE MAIN THEMES OF ANNA'S STORY

- Anna, a holy and wise woman, saw things that were not yet apparent to others: she saw the destiny of the small child Jesus when she held him in her arms.
- Like many stories in the New Testament, this is not about the woman Anna *but about Jesus*. Its purpose was to show *who Jesus is.*

It blows me away a lady at an old age Anna is still fasting and praying Luke 2:37 (NIV). You know she had to have *good health*.

It must had been so thrilling for Anna to hold baby Jesus. A long time waiting.

Anna shows wisdom, dedication, patience, she was holy, honorable and strong so many virtues are in one lady.

Here, in front of their eyes, is the Being who will bring redemption to Israel.

Do we feel unloved? Unworthy? Our Heavenly Father never sees us that way. Nothing can ever separate us from the love of God Ephesians 1:3–9 (ESV). No feeling. No thoughts. No attitude. No sin. No mistake can separate us from the love of God. You cannot escape His love. It is ever reaching to us.

For I am persuaded, that neither death, nor life, nor angels, nor principalities, nor powers, nor things present, nor things to come, Nor height, nor depth, nor any other creature, shall be able to separate us from the love of God... Romans 8 (KJV).

ARE WE LIVING FOR JESUS?

Are we Living for Jesus, does it show in all we do? Do we allow God's Holy Spirit, to guide us through? Are we living and growing Stronger in His grace? Will we see Him face to face?

As for me, I shall behold thy face in righteousness: I shall be satisfied, when I awake, with thy likeness. Psalm 17:15 (ESV).

All my life I thought we reaped *Curses* and *Blessings* that was given out in Deuteronomy. It was just recently through study I realized that Jesus had taken our curses away from us.

Christ hath redeemed us from the curse of the law, being made a curse for us... Galatians 3:13 (KJV).

We still obtain the *blessings* that are given through Abraham.

It is you who are the sons of the prophets and of the covenant which God made with your fathers, saying to **Abraham**, and in your seed all the families of the earth shall be **blessed**. Genesis 22:18 (KJV).

And I will make you a great nation, And I will bless you, And make your name great; And so you shall be a blessing; And I will bless those who bless you, And the one who curses you I will curse. And in you all the families of the earth will be blessed through you." Genesis 12:2-3 (NIV).

Studying the Word of God is a good thing. God will enlighten us with the words of God where things we didn't see before finally dawns on us.

God sent His own Son in the likeness of sinful flesh to be a sin offering. And so he condemned sin in the flesh, in order that the righteous requirement of the law might be fully met in us, who do not live according to the flesh but according to the Spirit.

After studying I realize a lot of things I was brought up with were not exactly true by the word of God.

It is our responsibility to find out 'what is what'. We must study and see what we believe in. If we don't we will follow what is not true according to God's word.

I have learned more in studying God's words to know what I believe in and wanting to tell others.

Everyone wants to make God mysterious... He is mysterious to a non-believer. But as a Christian the Bible tells us that the mystery of God is Jesus Christ: Ephesians 3:1-4 (KJV). My purpose is that they may be encouraged in heart and united in love, so that they may have the full riches of complete understanding, in order that they may know the mystery of God...

As the heavens are higher than the earth, so are my ways higher than your ways and my thoughts than your thoughts. Isaiah 55:9 (NIV).

This verse was given to the non-believer's not Christians.

When we accept Jesus Christ into our life we become righteous and our thoughts are God's thoughts.

And be not conformed to this world: but be ye transformed by the renewing of your mind, that ye may prove what is that good, and acceptable, and perfect, will of God. Romans 12:2 (KJV).

**[This word is between the Old Covenant
and the New Covenant.]**

I will give you a new heart and put a new spirit in you; I will remove from you your heart of stone and give you a heart of flesh. Ezekiel 36:26 (NIV).

For as high as the heavens are above the earth, So great is His lovingkindness toward those who fear Him. As far as the east is from the west, So far has He removed our transgressions from us. Just as a father has compassion on his children. Psalm 103:11-13 (NASB).

So great is his mercy toward us that fear him - To those who reverence and serve him. That is, His mercy is thus great in forgiving their offenses; in imparting grace; in giving us support and consolation.

If we are to serve the Lord and do his work, we must commit ourselves to righteous discipline.

I will sing of loyalty and of justice, to you, O Lord, I will sing. Lord, you who have set before me the prize of your high calling, turn me away from my self-indulgent life. Let me take up my cross and follow you. Read Psalm 101:1 A Psalm of David. I will sing of mercy and judgment: unto thee, O LORD, will I sing.

PSALM PRAYER

The Lord loves those who hate evil; he guards the lives of his faithful... Rejoice in the Lord, O you righteous, and give thanks to the holy name! Psalm 97:10,12 (NRSV).

I will be careful to lead a blameless life - when will you come to me? I will conduct the affairs of my house with a blameless heart. I will not look with approval on anything that is vile. I hate what faithless people do; I will have no part in it. The perverse of heart shall be far from me; I will have nothing to do with what is evil. Psalm 101:2-4 (NIV).

PSALM 51 – ONE OF THE GREATEST PRAYERS

This psalm is one of the greatest prayers of repentance in the Bible. This is where David pours out his heart in deep-felt repentance and confession after his adultery and having conspired to murder Bathsheba's husband, Uriah. He cries out, "Have mercy on me, O God, according to your unfailing love" Psalm 51:1 (NIV), and prays to God to "Wash me thoroughly from my iniquity, and cleanse me from my sin" Psalm 51:2 (NIV) and God does just that.

We can never get enough whispers of prayer. It is good to read examples of peoples words in the Bible.

GOD WORKS IN SILENCE

God is the friend of silence. See how nature – trees, flowers, grass- grows in silence; see the stars, the moon and the sun, how they move in silence.... We need silence. Silence is a source of great strength. God reigned in silence many years ago.

"I have much more to say to you, more than you can now bear." John 16:12 (NIV).

This evening the Lord whispered to me and said, "I inspire those in whom I love."

I came back in the room and told my husband. I said, "God said he inspires those in whom He loves."

He sorta gave me a blank stare and said, "yes He does."

God whispers to us out from nowhere. I was cleaning the aquarium when these words came to me.

I felt good when the words came forth.

I AM A CHILD OF GOD

Incline your ear, and come to Me. Hear, and your soul shall live; And I will make an everlasting covenant with you— The sure mercies of David. **Isa 55:3 (KJV).**

When we face a roadblock, when God stops us in our tracks, what should we do?

We are the makers of our destiny, but not the masters of our destiny.

First, acknowledge that we are not the masters of our own destinies.

We should learn from the people of Babel, and do the opposite. They were filled with pride, and a sense that they answered to no one and could do anything they decided to do.

"And they said, Go to, let us build us a city and a tower, whose top may reach unto heaven; and let us make us a name, lest we be scattered abroad upon the face of the whole earth. Genesis 11:4 (KJV).

When we face a roadblock in life, the first thing we must do is to realize a more positive way, and acknowledge to God, that we are *not* the masters of our own destinies.

GOD IS

God proved this fact to the people of Babel.

Go to, let us go down, and there confound their language, that they may not understand one another's speech. So the LORD scattered them abroad from thence upon the face of all the earth: and they left off to build the city. Genesis 11:7,8 (KJV).

Next, look up and seek God

Once we've acknowledged to God that He is the One in control of this world and of our lives, we must then yield to Him that control...by seeking Him and His direction for our next steps.

God is sovereign and therefore, in control of everything. The Lord could've made all people like clones or robots to do His every bidding without a second thought. However, He made us people of *free will* to make choices that will lead our destiny. What does 'Sovereignty' mean: It means being the ultimate source of all power, authority, and everything that exists. Only God can make those claims; therefore, it's **God's sovereignty**

that makes Him superior to all other gods and makes Him, and Him alone, worthy of worship.

When life suddenly changes--when we face a roadblock The only thing to do is to LOOK UP.

God is the only One who can order our steps and direct our path through the maze of life Only He knows what direction our lives will go.

God is the maker of Roadblocks to turn us around.

"IF WE CAN'T CHANGE the CIRCUMSTANCES, CHANGE OUR SELF"

We cannot choose what will happen to us, but we can choose what happens in us. That is, we can choose to have the right attitude, one in which we view challenges as opportunities instead of problems. **Choose to be Positive.**

Everyday is a new beginning and everyday is a New Year. Father shine your face upon us and help us to realize daily you are with us and your ear is in tune to us, your eye is ever watching over us, and when we do what is right, you will answer **Here I Am**.

Trusting God's love enough to consistently give ourself away in love to others. This is the great paradox/Secret to Emotional Health. "We will be emotionally healthy when others love us the way we want to be loved" but: "we will become more emotionally healthy as we learn to love others the way God *already loves us..*"

We cannot choose how we feel, *we can choose how to respond to our feelings. And choosing according to the truth rather than our feelings.* If we uncritically obey our feelings, we will injure our self (and others) emotionally, and we will become a slave to our deceitful and corrupting desires (bitterness ugliness, hatefulness etc). But if we make decisions based on the truth (to act in love) regardless of how we feel, we (and others) will be spared much emotional injury, we will reap emotional health--and our desire can actually be re-trained to desire the way of the truth (engaging, forgiving & affirming our spouse vs. withdrawing, punishing & criticizing). This is what Ps. 37:4 (NIV) means, and this is one of the most wonderful benefits of walking in God's *truth* over many years.

A Psalm of David. Fret not thyself because of evildoers, neither be thou envious against the workers of iniquity. For they shall soon be cut down like the grass, and wither as the green herb. Trust in the LORD, and do good; so shalt thou dwell in the land, and verily thou shalt be fed. Psalm 37:4 (KJV).

For the vision is yet for an appointed time, but it hasteth to the end, and shall not lie: though it tarry, wait for it; for it will surely come, it will not delay. Habakkuk 2:3 (KJV).

God has an appointed time to fulfill the visions, dreams and desires of our heart. Just because it has taken a long time or because we've tried and failed doesn't mean it's not going to happen. Don't give up on those dreams! Don't be complacent about pursuing what God has placed in our heart. Our God is a faithful God. No matter ...how long it's been, no matter how impossible things look, if we'll stay in Faith, our set time is coming.

Remember, every dream that's in our Heart, every promise that has taken root, GOD PUT IT THERE. Not only that, but He has every intention of bringing it to pass. Hold on to that vision today. Declare by faith, "My time is coming. God is working behind the scenes on our behalf. I will fulfill my Destiny!" As we continue to hold on to that vision and speak life over our dreams, it won't be long before we see them begin to take shape. We'll see our faith grow, we'll see our hope strengthen, and we'll see our self step into the destiny God has prepared for us! Give him Thanks for what we are pursuing in advance be like Jehoshaphat where he sent his praisers out before the battle began and God turned the situation around and made the armies argue with themselves and Jehoshaphat didn't have to fight the armies – Jehoshaphat appointed men to sing to the LORD and to Praise Him for the Splendor of his Holiness as they went out at the head of the army, saying:

"Give Thanks to the LORD,
for his Love Endures Forever."

Then, led by Jehoshaphat, all the men of Judah and Jerusalem returned Joyfully to Jerusalem, for the LORD had given them cause to Rejoice Over their enemies. II Chron 20:27-30 (NIV).

Have Faith approach God in Praise and Thank Him for the new job, the new beginning, the strength to stand strong against circumstances, *everything we need praise him in advance* – our eyes cannot see but, God is working the best for us.

"Not that I speak in respect of want: for I have learned, in whatsoever state I am, therewith to be content.." Philippians 4:11 (NIV).

In life, sometimes it's easy to get so focused on our dreams and goals that we tune out everything else. We can get to the point where we're not going to be happy until we see those things happen. But I've found that if we have to have something in order to be happy, our lives are out of balance. When our goals and dreams start to frustrate us, and we lose our... peace and don't enjoy life, that's a clear sign that we're holding on too tightly. What's the solution? We've got to release it. Freedom comes when we say, "God, I'm turning it all over to you. You know my desires and what's best for me. I'm choosing to trust You and Your timing." When we learn to be content whatever the circumstances, it takes away the power of the enemy. Our actions, are showing our faith in God. *When we choose to trust His timing, we can live in peace,* we can live in joy, and we can rest in Him knowing that He has good things in store for our future. Today, find freedom in contentment and rest in His everlasting peace — Philippians 4:11 (NASB) - "What does God give us strength to do? Everything means all that God desires us to do – not absurd, selfish or evil things. In Paul's own example, it meant that God had given him the ability to be content whether he had plenty or overwhelming need. God's grace will sustain us not matter where he leads – even when we lack of material things." Christ who is the secret of Paul's serenity – The presence of God, who shows us by the cross of Christ that he is for us, not against us, and that he was so filled with love for us that he sent his Son to die on our behalf.

There's a whole bunch of promises in Deuteronomy 28. The promises are based on obedience to the law of God. (ten commandments are our guideline) As *New Covenant believers,* the promises of Deuteronomy 28 are available to us because of Jesus' obedience in fulfilling the law. Because He fulfilled the law completely, we have access to every promise and we are free of every curse. Our children are blessed, our career is blessed, our household is blessed, and wherever we go is blessed.

Our children are given Peace.

"I will teach all your children, and they will enjoy great peace." Isaiah 54:13 (NLT).

The Lord teaches our children. His ways surpasses exceeds greater than anything. The children are taught of the Lord. And as a result, they experience *Peace*. Not fear. Not discouragement. Not distress. But Peace.

I tell my daughter God is faithful. We need to pray with them and let them know our relationship with God.

Put the Promise to work

THANK YOU LORD

We dwell upon the goodness in our life. We cherish in our heart Your gift to us. Thank You. We notice the blessings of life, Thank You, Lord.

BE KIND
EVEN ON OUR
BAD DAYS

ACT OF HOPE

O My God, relying on Thy almighty power and infinite mercy and promises, we thank You that You have pardon of our sins, the help of thy grace, and life everlasting, through the merits of Jesus Christ, our Lord and redeemer amen.

The Love of God surrounds us - Like the air we breathe – As near as a heartbeat as close as a whispered prayer. Whenever we need Him He'll always be there.

Your kingdom is an everlasting kingdom, and your dominion endures through all generations. Psalm 145:13 (KJV).

The LORD is trustworthy in all he promises and faithful in all he does.

"Inner peace is the key: if you have inner peace, the external problems do not affect your deep sense of peace and tranquility."

"Peace I leave with you; My peace I give to you; not as the world gives do I give to you. Do not let your heart be troubled, neither let it be afraid." John 14:27 (NIV).

"And let the Peace (Soul Harmony which comes) from Christ rule (act as umpire continually) in your Hearts [deciding and settling with finality all questions that arise in your Minds, in that Peaceful state] to which as [members of Christ's] one body you were also called [to live]. And be Thankful (Appreciative), [Giving Praise to God Always]." Colossians 3:15 (AMP).

An umpire calls the players safe or out. As believers in Jesus, we have an internal umpire, so to speak, calling the plays and giving us direction. Before we ever make a decision, we should stop and see if we have Peace inside. If there's unrest or an uneasy feeling inside, then don't move forward. Let Peace be our umpire. How many people get into a relationship that they didn't have Peace and end up miserable? I've been there. They buy things they didn't have Peace about. They end up in debt. They take a job they didn't have Peace about. They end up frustrated. Here's the key: If we don't have Peace before we make the decision, we're not going to have Peace after we make the decision. If we don't have Peace about that person now, we are not going to have Peace if we get into a relationship. If we don't have Peace about buying that new car, we are not going to have Peace when the payments come each month. Remember, God gave us Peace for our *Protection*. No matter what circumstances look like, always Trust God's inner Peace. Let Peace in our Heart be our Umpire and settle any questions we have in our mind.

PRAYER FOR STRENGTH

God surround us, let Your Peace be ours, Keep us safe in Your arms. God thank You for your cleansing power. For we have new life again because of Your Son God be beside us, as we walk hand in hand, filling our mind with new songs and plans.

Thank You Lord for being within us, restoring our soul. In Christ Jesus we pray. amen.

KEEP YOUR HEART WITH ALL DILIGENCE

"Keep your Heart with all Diligence, For out of it Spring the Issues of Life." Proverbs 4:23-27 (NKJV).

In this life we will witness great misfortune and injustice but we can't allow it to Steal our Hopes. In the end of this age God will set all things right. We must shield our hearts with this Hope that our 'Joy' might remain full and we don't become sad and down cast. We allow disobedience to overthrow our Hope that our Hearts become hardened and we lose faith in God's Sovereignty. When we doubt God's Sovereignty we are apt to take things into our own hands and that can produce death. We guard our hearts to keep seeds of doubt, unbelief, fear, hatred and other evils from being sown into it. Let the words in John 16:33 (NIV) as spoken by Jesus before His crucifixion always strengthen us. "I have told you these things, so that in me you may have Peace. In this world you will have trouble. But take heart! I have overcome the world."

Can we say of the creator that set the seasons in their time, and the moon phases in its time, day and night in their time, and even gestation (carrying of young in the uterus: pregnancy conception and development especially in the mind) in its time, that His timing is off pertaining to the circumstances in our life How can we not trust God's timing? God's timing is perfect and His timing sustains our life.

"Wait for the LORD; be strong and take heart and wait for the LORD.." Psalm 27:14 (NIV).

Sometimes we have to wait for our seasoned time.

"They that wait upon the Lord shall renew their strength; they shall mount up with wings as eagles; they shall run, and not be weary; and they shall walk, and not faint." Isaiah 40:31 (KJV).

We live in a world of instant gratification. But if you look at nature, nature doesn't rush things. Babies, human, furry, and otherwise, all have their allotted time of gestation.

The mother is in a time of waiting. She is not, however, idle. She is eating well, taking care of herself, and making the necessary preparations for a new life.

In order to grow tall, a tree needs good soil, water, and sunshine. It needs to establish a strong root system so that it can grow as tall as it can. It needs strong roots to withstand the winds and rains. Growth takes time. You cannot rush growth. Rushing goes against nature. It goes *against our spiritual growth* too.

Waiting is trusting. When we trust, we let go of the anxiety that comes with waiting. It's self-induced suffering. Don't allow anxiety and stress to fill moments when you must wait.

The apostle Paul said, "We know that all things work together for good for those who love God, who are called according to his purpose." Romans 8:28 (NIV).

When I look back on my life, I can see how all the experiences brought me to where I am today. Circumstances were not always very good at the time, however, things worked together for good. *Much of that time was waiting for my life to unfold.*

A song dear to my Heart
I'D RATHER HAVE JESUS

I'd rather have Jesus than silver or gold
I'd rather be His than have riches untold
I'd rather have Jesus than houses or land
I'd rather be led by His nail-pierced hand

Than to be the king of a vast domain or be held in sins dread sway
I'd rather have Jesus than anything
This world affords today...
by Rhea F. Miller

There are always beautiful songs that linger forever. Such as; I'd rather have Jesus, or They that wait upon the Lord. My mother and father would sing these two songs as I was growing up with my father playing the acoustic guitar. I would hold very still to listen to them to sing. I enjoyed it so much.

My dad was a minister of The Church of God and Pentecostal religions and as I watch some of his ministry I will never forget how he would get so stirred up when he ministered about the **The Valley of Dry Bones** coming back to life again. see Ezekiel 37.

"This is what the Lord GOD says to these bones: I will cause breath to enter you, and you will live. I will attach tendons to you and make flesh come upon you and cover you with skin; I will put breath in you, and you will come to life. Then you will know that I am the LORD." Ezekiel 37:5-6 (NIV).

When I watched him it was God's spirit taking over his whole body. With so much eagerness, enthusiasm, with sincerity that came forth in his message.

Breath came into the bones and they lived. God made dead bones rise to life, and He did this by giving to the bones His live-giving breath.

"He that believeth in Me, though he were dead, yet shall he live" John 11:25 (KJV). For He will open the old graves of our dead hearts, and raise our souls into spiritual life. And, in this, our Lord will fulfill, spiritually, the promise of our text, "O My people, I will open your graves, and cause you to come up out of your graves, and bring you into the land of Israel." Ezekiel 37:12 (KJV).

Note: A lot of the people had died in a foreign land. Commentary states The Valley of the Dry Bones represents the unregenerate vs the regenerate hearts.

Even though my biblical ways are not my natural father's ways. I did get the *theory of salvation* breaded in me. Even though the views of salvation differ. My *salvation* is irrevocable and you can not lose God's irrevocable gift. Even though I had to find my own purposeful journey through Christ who draws me to Him.

Remember we come to Christ through and by God drawing us not us choosing him.

"No one can come to me unless the Father who sent me draws them, and I will raise them up at the last day. John 6:44 (NIV).

JESUS THE BREAD
OF LIFE

66 "Stop grumbling among yourselves," Jesus replied. "No one can come to Me unless the Father who sent Me draws him, and I will raise him up at the last day. Read John 6:43-51 (NIV). It is written in the Prophets: And they will all be taught by God. Everyone who has heard the Father and learned from Him comes to Me—...

My natural father did his job to the best of his God given ability. In his house no cussing, no taking God's name in vain, prayers before everything even before we opened up Christmas gifts giving Thanks unto the Father. He was a prime example of giving our heavenly Father His reverence.

My husband does the same thing. He puts God first of giving Thanks before our meals. When he tries to quote a scripture and messes up he asks the Father to forgive him. Then he goes and searches for that word to speak it rightly.

I am very well pleased when he corrects himself. He is a person where God deals with his heart immediately. Immediately Patrick takes it to the Lord in whispers of prayer.

Reverencing the Lord is important sometimes we fall. By being at a friend's house and not reverencing at the time to eat. Recently this happened and we both felt bad. I felt funny to eat without prayer. I had to ask the heavenly Father for forgiveness of lack of reverence.

To worship God is to know Him and to serve Him. To worship Him the way He deserves to be worshiped, *we must align our hearts* with His and *seek to obey Him.*

"Why do you call me, 'LORD, LORD,' and do not do what I say? Luke 6:46 (KJV).

REVERENCE

✝

Reverence starts in the heart and manifests in the actions. In the Bible, we are frequently instructed to reverence God, which can also be phrased as honoring or fearing God. I Samuel 12:34 (KJV) says: "Only fear the LORD and serve him faithfully with all your heart. For consider what great things he has done for you." When we have reverence for God, it manifests in our actions as **obedience** and **praise** to Him.

Having reverence for God means that we acknowledge His lordship in 'every area of our lives and we obey' what He commands.

Whispers of Prayer from a
Reverence Heart

While He was on earth, Jesus was heard by God "because of His *reverence*," which lets us know that God will also hear us when we *pray* from a *heart of reverence*. Hebrews 5:7 (NIV).

When we recognize God's ultimate holiness and combine that with recognizing His *goodness* and *faithfulness* to us, the only natural response we can have is to worship Him He is worthy of all praise. We thank Him for the saving grace He has provided for us, receive His love, and acknowledge Him as the omnipotent God of all.

Every good and perfect gift is from above, coming down from the Father of the heavenly lights, who does not change like shifting shadows. James 1:17 (NIV).

Unlike man who changes from one day to the next, God is immutable and unchanging, which means He is absolutely reliable and trustworthy Malachi 3:6 (NASB); I the LORD do not change. Numbers 23:19 (NIV); God is not human, that he should lie... Psalm 102:27 (NIV) ...remain the same..

JESUS CRUSHED SATAN

Satan can be rendered *powerless* in our life
Jesus crushed Satan under His feet

T he God of peace will *soon crush Satan under your feet.* The Grace of our Lord Jesus be with you. Romans 16:20 (NIV).

Crushed can only mean that his destructive power will be rendered completely ineffective in our life!

We won't find stronger words than these! Greater words do not exist! But the greatest and best thing about these words is that they are true. Satan misleads, harms, dominates, and destroys all who will let themselves be misled, harmed, dominated, and destroyed – that is, all who have not received grace to resist his power. When he is crushed under your feet, then his misleading and destructive power is crushed as far as you are concerned, so he is no longer able to cause you to fall. He has no more power over you. Jesus said, "All things are possible to him who believes." Mark 9:23 (KJV).

Notice in Romans 16:20 (NIV), that it is the God of peace who crushes Satan under our feet. That might seem to be a disjunction; what does peace have to do with crushing? But that is exactly how God has given us His peace—Jesus crushed the head of the evil one and destroyed all his works. The work of the devil is *to steal, kill and destroy,* but *Jesus came to give us His peace,* the *life* of God in *abundance* John 10:10 (ESV).

If Jesus came to *destroy* the works of the devil, then why are people still claiming His presence today? Because God is not only doing a work in and for His people, He is doing a work through His people. Jesus has delivered the *death blow* to *Satan* and *all His works,* but He has given His people the authority and power to *enforce* that *victory* over the adversary: "Behold, I give you the authority to trample on serpents and scorpions, and over all the power of the enemy, and nothing shall by any means hurt you." Luke 10:19 (KJV).

Jesus has not only given us authority, but power also, just as He promised: "You shall receive power when the Holy Spirit has come upon you" Acts 1:8 (NIV). This is the same power by which *Jesus performed all His miracles and destroyed the works of the devil:* "God anointed Jesus of Nazareth with the Holy Spirit and with power, who went about doing good and healing all who were *oppressed by the devil*, for God was with Him" Acts 10:38 (ESV*). The broken power of the devil is no match against the power of the Holy Spirit.*

When God raised Jesus from the dead by the power of the Holy Spirit… The *Power of death*, the *last enemy*, is *broken.*

Then the end will come, when *he hands over the kingdom* to God the Father after he has destroyed *all dominion, authority and power.* I Corinthians 15:24 (NIV).

God is crushing Satan under our feet. He has given us authority to trample on the power and works of the enemy. Just as these things are under the feet of Jesus, they are under our feet as well. For we are His body, the fullness of Him. Not only that, but the Bible says that, just as Jesus is seated in the Heaven-lies at the right hand of the Father, we are also seated there in Him. God has "made us alive together with Christ (by grace you have been saved), and raised us up together, and made us sit together in the heavenly places in Christ Jesus".

made us alive with Christ even when we were dead in transgressions—it is by grace you have been saved. Ephesians 2:5-6 (NIV).

God is putting all things under the feet of Jesus, and you and I get to be a part of that victory. As believers in Jesus Christ, we no longer have to listen to the lies and accusations of the devil, or be subject to his power, for that power has been broken and has no authority, and no ability, to rule over us and Satan can not read our minds. We are part of the body of Christ. We are now part of that fullness which fills all in all. The term "God's right hand" in prophecy refers to the Messiah to whom is given the power and authority to subdue His enemies....this that is the *outworking of His Peace, His Shalom, in the world.* If Satan could read minds then he would had read Jobs mind knowing Job wasn't going to denounce His God.

The only power Satan has in the life of a believer is the power *we allow* him to have, by *our own disobedience.* James had the answers we need to walk in victory and keep Satan under our feet.

The devil is already conquered, and his works are destroyed, then why are so many afraid of him, and believe that he has the power to make you sin?

The devil is defeated, Jesus defeated him Colossians 2:15 (NIV). ...And having disarmed the powers and authorities, he made a public spectacle of them, triumphing over them by the cross. "Having spoiled principalities and powers, He made a show of them openly, triumphing over them in it".

The LORD said unto my Lord, Sit thou at my right hand, until I make thine enemies thy footstool.; Psalm 118:16 (NIV). The Lord's right hand is lifted high; the Lord's right hand has done mighty things!". Psalm 110:1 (KJV).

Let us as Christians have the knowledge of God and let God direct our life today and not be ignorant to his word. Be not deceived and take up your bed and follow the only wise God our Savior.

How does Satan get power over people? He simply entices them to commit sin. Once they have committed sin, he accuses them day and night. They get a bad conscience and lose their peace, joy, power, and boldness and are separated from God. By our own disobedience causes circumstances to take place because we have put iniquity/sins between us and God. God allows circumstances to take place in our life to help us turn around.

When we whisper prayer and have sin in our life, we pray **Amiss** prayer where God doesn't hear us. We must ask for the forgiveness of sin and purify our self before asking anything of God. Amiss is harboring sin in our hearts. See James 4:1-3 (KJV).

Submit yourselves therefore to God. Resist the devil, and he will flee from you. Draw nigh to God, and he will draw nigh to you. Cleanse your hands, you sinners; and purify your hearts, you double minded. Be afflicted, and mourn, and weep: let your laughter be turned to mourning, and your joy to heaviness. Humble yourselves in the sight of the Lord, and he shall lift you up. James 4:7-10 (NIV).

PRAY
WAIT
TRUST

AARON'S BLESSING

The LORD bless you, and keep you; The LORD make His face shine on you, And be gracious to you; The LORD lift up His countenance on you, And give you peace. Number 6:24 (NIV).

PRAYER FOR STRENGTH

You are my strength Jesus. Help me to carry Your responsibilities with grace. I will lift each worry or burden to You. Help me to defend truth, justice and righteousness in everything. Thank You. In Christ Jesus, amen.

God wants the wicked to Repent
Christians quote scripture texts out of Context

God calls Israel to repentance. If they repent, God will make a covenant with them. Read Exodus 24. They will be a strong nation whom can command other nations to action. God will be their God and they will be God's people.

But as of now, there is a problem. The people are wicked, so wicked that they risk being punished in spite of any repentance. It is this that God tries to dispel:

Let the wicked forsake his way, And the unrighteous man his thoughts; Let him return to the LORD, And He will have mercy on him; And to our God, For He will abundantly pardon. Isa 55:7 (KJV).

The following Verses Isa 55:8-9 (KJV) are given to the non-believer's.

"For My thoughts are not your thoughts, Nor are your ways My ways," says the LORD. Isaiah 55:8 (KJV).

"For as the heavens are higher than the earth, So are My ways higher than your ways, And My thoughts than your thoughts. Isaiah 55:9 (KJV).

God wants the wicked to repent. It is them to whom God says "my thoughts are not your thoughts." It is that person whom God will pardon, because "God's ways are not His ways." Normal people, especially the wicked audience of this chapter, would not pardon as God does. But God promises blessings for the wicked if they repent.

God then proceeds to detail His promise of blessings.

So shall My word be that goes forth from My mouth; It shall not return to Me void, But it shall accomplish what I please, And it shall prosper in the thing for which I sent it. Isaiah 55:11 (KJV).

God will create prosperity without His work returning fruitless. This is the context of God's word not returning to Him void.

God then paints a picture of the paradise He is promising:

"For you shall go out with joy, And be led out with peace; The mountains and the hills shall break forth into singing before you, and all the trees of the field shall clap their hands." Isaiah 55:12 (NKJV).

"Instead of the thorn shall come up the cypress tree, and instead of the brier shall come up the myrtle tree; and it shall be to the LORD for a name, for an everlasting sign that shall not be cut off." Isa 55:13 (ESV).

TODAY

Today, as our thoughts of God enter our heart, worries will leave.

But my eyes are toward you, O God, my Lord; in you I seek refuge; leave me not defenseless! Psalm 141:8-10 (ESV).

Todays each beat of our heart will remind us that God is with us.

THANKFUL
AND
GRATEFUL

I was in question about tithing after one evening my husband I went to church on a Wednesday evening. We were fresh newbies. We were giving a lot of money from our pockets in the tithing envelope but we weren't putting it in as a tithe. We put it in the envelope as a gift since we weren't a member. This one particular evening we enter church and to our surprise the whole church was laid out as a banquet hall with white linings, candelabra's of beauty. We questioned what is going on? The person said, "there was no service this particular evening." Only tithe payers were invited to a dinner this particular evening. This was a secretive invite. Others that attended the church weren't invited and no service that night. We were very much offended and hurt. I had to research tithing to know the outcome and this is my finds.

'TITHING'

Bring the whole tithe into the storehouse, that there may be food in my house. Test me in this says the Lord Almighty, and see if I will not throw open the floodgates of heaven and pour out so much blessing that you will not have room enough for it. I will prevent pests from devouring your crops, and the vines in your field will not cast their fruit says the Lord Almighty Malachi 3:10-11 (NIV).

"Return to me and I will return to you" Malachi 3:7 (NIV). The old covenant is not an eternal covenant nor mandate upon the human race – it was given to Israel, and Israel-only, to be a unique, set-apart-people to God…) The old covenant replacement with the new and far better covenant did not abolished the laws of God! What was abolished were the rituals and to the letter penalties of transgressing the laws of God. Think without the law there would be no sin! The law is to be established not only in our hearts but in our communities literally-in thoughts, in words and in deeds! The accompanying sacrificial, ceremonial injunctions have ceased but not the dietary & civil ones. However the Civil Laws punishment and penalties is now up to God to punish with Him now being among us (Emmanuel) and because of His Grace; and us being ministers of the spirit and not the letter! The dietary law's transgression have consequences spiritually and physically…

so does the transgression on the tithe, marriage, sabbaths, feasts days and even when not obeying God's laws on agriculture!

We are not lawless however, for the (moral elements) of the law are written on our Hearts – the Holy Spirit convicts us of sin… But the tithe is no longer mandated upon the believer – even the council in Acts 15 mentioned nothing about tithing upon Gentiles… Paul never preached tithing to either his Jewish or Gentile converts, and with the eventual separation of the Jewish Believers from the Synagogues and the Temple, no longer did they tithe per the mandates of the Old Covenant. ***Well we are under Grace and not under the Law,*** and God knows what each one of us have in our Hearts. Whether we really understand what we are doing and teaching this is what the Lord Jesus have to say. (NOTE: If you are going to a Church and they want you to tithe check upon your heart to give what God would have you to give – I do think we need to support our church so that it can function properly. Listen to our heart. We need to have a personal relationship with the Lord that gives us peace about whether we should tithe.

Although there are many preachers and denominations that teach that Christians should tithe (give 10% of their income) to their churches, there is no scriptural basis for this. From the beginning, Christianity broke apart from the 614 laws of the OT, especially among gentiles. Yet, many preachers teach that this is the one law that we must keep. Meanwhile:

1. The scripture always speaks of the tithe as food, never money. See Matthew 23:23 (NIV).
2. The first tithe was a customary offering to Melchizedek for protection as Abraham crossed his land. See Genesis 14.

3. Jacob was actually command to EAT his tithe. See Genesis 28:20-22 (NIV).
4. The tithe of Israel was designed to sustain the Levite priests, who ceased to operate in seventy (70) AD when the temple was destroyed. Jews have not tithed since.
5. The church did not teach tithe until the 700s AD, when the religion needed a boost to propagate into a political power.
6. Jesus distributed the priesthood to all believers and even called them the temple. If the tithe belongs with anyone it is the individual believers. I Peter 2:9 (NIV).
7. The authority to demand or collect tithes was never assigned to an institution.
8. New Testament giving was never to be done under compulsion.

Therefore, any church teaching that tithes are required of Christians is robbing the believers of their wages and using it to advance its own agenda. Mostly to pay for their expensive, unscriptural model of the institutional church.

"A tithe of everything from the land, whether grain from the soil or fruit from the trees, belongs to the LORD; it is holy to the LORD. Whoever would redeem any of their tithe must add a fifth of the value to it. Every tithe of the herd and flock-every tenth animal that passes under the shepherd's rod-will be holy to the LORD. No one may pick out the good from the bad or make any substitution. If anyone does make a substitution, both the animal and its substitute become holy and cannot be redeemed." These are the commands the LORD gave Moses at Mount Sinai for the Israelites. Leviticus 27:30-34 (NIV).

These nations carried on very corrupt, idolatrous forms of worship and immoral practices beastiality. God had commanded Israel to clean them out of the land. See Leviticus 18:24,28 (NIV).

NEW COVENANT FREEDOM

In the Old Covenant tithing was required. That's no longer the case for us as part of the New Covenant because we are free from the curse of the law.

Therefore there is no punishment associated with not tithing. Instead, when we choose to tithe *from our own free will*, it releases God to be able to actively act on our behalf in two very specific ways. He can then open up additional heavenly blessings into our lives and our finances. And he can act on our behalf to prohibit the devourer from wasting away our finances.

We absolutely do not have to tithe. God will still love us just as much whether we tithe or not.

But now that we know the benefits God promises if we do tithe, why would we not want to enjoy those extra blessings?

We can give in many other ways because God loves a cheerful giver.

do not worry about your life

Therefore I tell you, do not worry about your life, what you will eat or drink; or about your body, what you will wear. Is not life more than food, and the body more than clothes? Matthew 6 (NIV).

There is scarcely any sin against which our Lord Jesus more warns his disciples, than disquieting, distracting, distrustful cares about the things of this life. This often in snares the poor as much as the love of wealth does the rich. But there is a carefulness about temporal things which is a duty, though we must not carry these lawful cares too far. Take no thought for our life. Not about the length of it; but refer it to God to lengthen or shorten it as he pleases; our times are in his hand, and they are in a good hands. Not about the comforts of this life; but leave it to God to make it bitter or sweet as he pleases. Food and raiment God has PROMISED, therefore we may expect them. Take no thought for the morrow, for the time to come. Be not anxious for the future, how we shall live next year, or when we are old, or what we shall leave behind us. As we must not boast of tomorrow, so we must not care for to-morrow, or the events of it. God has given us life, and has given us the body. And what can he not do for us, who did that? If we take care about our souls and for eternity, which are more than the body and its life, we may leave it to God to provide for us food and raiment, which are less. Improve this as an encouragement to TRUST God. We must reconcile ourselves to our worldly estate, as we do to our stature. We cannot alter the disposals of providence, therefore we must submit and resign ourselves to them. Thoughtfulness for our souls is the best cure of thoughtfulness for the world. Seek first the kingdom of God, and make Christianity your business: say not that this is the way to starve; no, it is the way to be well provided for, even in this world. The conclusion of the whole matter is, that it is the Will and Command of the Lord Jesus, that by daily whispers of prayers we may get strength to bear us up under our daily troubles, and to arm us against the influences that attend them, and then let none of these things move us. *Happy are those who take the Lord for their God*, and make full proof of it by trusting themselves wholly to his wise disposal. Let thy Spirit convince us of sin in the want of this disposition, and take away the worldliness of our hearts.

Give Thanks to the Lord, for He is Good

...How blessed are those who keep Justice, Who practice Righteousness at all times! Remember me, O LORD, in Your Favor toward Your people; visit me with your salvation, that I may see the prosperity of your chosen ones, that I may rejoice in the gladness of Your nation, that I may glory with your inheritance... Psalm 106:3-5 (NASB).

Whispers of Prayer for Change

Indeed, this is our confidence: Anything we whisper in prayer that aligns with the Father's plan will be granted. And the more time we spend with Him, the more we'll come to understand His will and how to pray for it.

Remember, **prayer doesn't change God's mind, but it does transform the believer's heart**. Some requests are granted immediately, simply because we asked with the realization that our Father loves to give us good gifts. Other requests may require time or certain divine preparations before they can be given. We, meanwhile, must simply be diligent to persevere in whispers of prayer.

Whatever the Lord's response or timing, we trust that He has only the very best in store for His children. That means we might not receive exactly what we're asking for, but something even better. Such is God's great pleasure, for **He alone perfectly knows each heart's desire and wishes to fulfill it**.

"The LORD be magnified, *Who delights in the prosperity of His servant.*" Psalm 35:27 (NASB). David prays, My soul is in danger, Lord, rescue it; it belongs to thee the Father of spirits, therefore claim thine own; it is thine, save it! Lord, be not far from me, as if I were a stranger. We must trust our souls in God's hands, which are one with him by faith, are precious in his sight, and shall be rescued from destruction, that we may give thanks in heaven.

CIRCUMSTANCES AND HEARING GOD'S VOICE

When considering how God uses circumstances to guide us, we should consider the balance of two truths: first, God can and does use *circumstances* to guide us into His Will; and second, *circumstances* are not always an indication of God's plan for our lives. We approach God's truth in a balanced fashion, weighing the scriptures and opinions on both ends of an issue. It is probably easier to be swayed by *circumstances* than by any of the other keys to God's guidance. *Circumstances* are so real to us in the physical world. Anything that touches our person in this world is *circumstance* - joy, sorrow, hunger, pain, happiness, cold, heat, birth, death. When it comes to being led through *circumstances*. God does lead His children in many different ways: through scripture, by speaking directly to our spirit, through godly counsel, and through other supernatural guidance like personal prophecy, signs, dreams, visions, and in any way God sees fit. The truth is that we are a spirit, we have a soul, and we live in a body. God can and will communicate with all aspects of who we are. He will use every means necessary to reach us with His message of love and grace.

God *is* Love - *and* LOVES *to* communicate

God will often use the so-called closed doors in our life to mold our character and prepare us for our next step. Maturity comes to believers when they allow the Holy Spirit to break them of their vulnerability to *circumstances* in life. A Teacher Larry Tomczak, said, "You're not under the *circumstances;* you're above the *circumstances.* You're not contending with the devil for a place of victory; you overcome the devil from your position of victory.

Circumstances, taken apart from consideration of the scriptures and the peace of God, can lead us astray. We can learn to discern God's hand in both *positive* and *negative circumstances.* But neither favorable nor unfavorable *circumstances* can be taken alone as a sign that we are in or out of the will

of God. Understanding our situation and try to evaluate our situation we must consult God and allow him to lead. That is why it is important at early morning put everything into the hands of God and when we do God takes the driver's seat. If we have a situation that calls for a decision get God's Peace first.

HAVE WE OPENED THE BOOK?
The book of beginnings, it's new life given free.

The treasures of the heart we will find are not hidden but are manifested through the Word. God says, His words are medicine.

A joyful heart is good medicine, But a broken spirit dries up the bones. Proverbs 17:22 (NASB).

JESUS IS MY PORTION MY CONSTANT FRIEND IS HE

HE DELIGHTS IN OUR PROSPERITY

"Let them shout for joy, and be glad, that favour my righteous cause: yea, let them say continually, Let the LORD be magnified, which hath pleasure in the prosperity of his servant." Psalm 35:27 (KJV).

God desires that we be blessed and prosperous in all that we do! He desires that we be so blessed that we can turn around and be a blessing everywhere we go. He wants us to have so much peace, joy and victory that when other people get around us, it spills over onto them. In the Psalm, David said, "My Cup Runs Over." Psalm 23:5 (NKJV). He was saying, "I'm so full of God, I'm Overflowing! David prays, My soul is in danger, Lord, rescue it; it belongs to thee the Father of spirits, therefore claim thine own; it is thine, save it! Read Psalm 35 (KJV). Lord, be not far from me, as if I were a stranger. He who exalted the once suffering redeemer, will appear for all his people: the roaring lion shall not destroy their souls, any more than he could that of Christ, their surety. They trust their souls in his hands, one with him by faith, are precious in his sight, and shall be rescued from destruction, that they may give *thanks* in heaven.

Don't settle for a barely-get-by-mentality (which we all have lived) I call it a wilderness mentality. Jesus came so that we can live an abundant life. That means an Abundance of Joy, an Abundance of Peace, an Abundance of Health, an Abundance of meeting our finances. We may not see it right now, and maybe we haven't experienced it in the past, but don't get satisfaction and just settle where we are. Get a vision for our future! Get a vision for what God wants to do in our life — God delights in our prosperity! See Psalm 35:27 (KJV). We can have no nobler title than Servant of God, and no greater reward than for our Master to delight in our prosperity. What true prosperity may be we are not always best able to judge. We must leave that in Jesus' hand; he will not fail to rule all things for our highest good!

PRAYER

"Father, thank You for Your hand of blessing on our life. Help us develop a vision for the abundant life You have in store and show us how to be a blessing everywhere we go in Christ Jesus, amen.

HOPE

Of all of God's wonderful blessings hope keeps a song in our heart brings pleasure to our soul, gives us the assurance all is well as we wait for our 'victory'.

PRAY WITHOUT CEASING

Paul's command in I Thessalonians 5:17 (KJV) to *"pray without ceasing,"* can be confusing. Obviously, it cannot mean we are to be in a head-bowed, eyes-closed posture all day long. Paul is not referring to non-stop talking, but rather an attitude of *God-consciousness* and *God-surrender that we carry with us all the time.* Every waking moment is to be lived in an awareness that God is with us and that He is actively involved and engaged in our thoughts and actions.

When our thoughts turn to worry, fear, discouragement, and anger, we are to consciously and quickly turn every thought into prayer and every prayer into thanksgiving. In his letter to the Philippians, Paul commands us to stop being anxious and instead, *"in everything,* by prayer and petition, with thanksgiving, present your requests to God" Philippians 4:6 (NIV). He taught the believers at Colossae to devote themselves "to prayer, being watchful and thankful" Colossians 4:2 (NLT) Devote yourselves to prayer with an alert mind and a thankful heart.). Paul exhorted the Ephesians believers to see prayer as a weapon to use in fighting spiritual battles Ephesians 6:18 (NIV). As we go through the day, prayer should be our first response to every fearful situation, every anxious thought, and every undesired task that God commands. A lack of whispers of prayer will *cause us to depend on ourselves instead of depending on God's Grace*. Unceasing Prayer is, in essence, Continual Dependence upon and Communion with the Father.

DEFINITIONS OF PROSPERITY

God said he delights in our prosperity...

Level #0. <u>Egypt living</u> - This is Bondage. This is where a person is Broke, cannot pay their bills they have not received a spoken blessing and they are living in poverty. Poverty is Bondage. ***The Bible even describes poverty as being a curse.*** (living in bondage is not for Christians we are not to be living in bondage - **Christ had taken bondage away** - Galatians 5:1 (KJV) Stand fast therefore in the liberty by which Christ has made us free, and do not be entangled again with a yoke of bondage.

Poverty is a Curse. It is important that we realize from reading the Bible that God considers poverty to be a curse. We find this to be true when we look at Job's story.

Level #1 <u>Wilderness living</u> - These are people that have come out of poverty but are still living day to day week-to-week and month-to-month. Bills are getting paid, important needs are being met but there is no money left over and no money to be a blessing or to provide for furthering the Kingdom of God. Most Christians live here.

Level #2 <u>**The Promised land**</u> - All bills are paid all needs are met according to God's Riches in glory by Christ Jesus. Finances are increasingly and have been blessed. Some Christians live here.

Level #3 <u>**The Abundant life**</u> - Jesus said in John 10:10 (NRSV) I am come that you might have life and have it more abundantly. The word abundantly when translated from the Greek means excessive, in excess. This means a life of more than enough. God is not only a God of enough; God is a God of Too Much. That's why David said in Psalm 23 (KJV) my cup runs over. My question is this; doesn't God know when the cup is full? The reason David's cup runs over is because that's the kind of God he served. A God of TOO MUCH!

This is where <u>God wants all of His people to be.</u>

May those who delight in my vindication shout for joy and gladness; may they always say, "The LORD be exalted, who delights in the well-being **of** his servant." Psalm 35:27 (NIV).

GOD'S DEFINITION OF PROSPERITY

In 2 Corinthians 9:8 (ESV) the Bible tells us and God is able to make all grace abound toward you; that you will always have all *sufficiency* in all things and may abound to every good work. John 10:10 (KJV) Jesus said the thief comes to steal, kill and to destroy I AM COME THAT THEY MIGHT HAVE A MORE ABUNDANT LIFE. Second Corinthians 8:9 (NIV) for you know the Grace of our Lord Jesus Christ, that though he was rich, yet for your sake he became poor, that you, through His Poverty might be Rich. This is part of the Divine Exchange. The other two parts are second Corinthians 5:21 (KJV) where Jesus took our sin so that we could become the righteousness of God through him.

And, I Peter 2:24 (KJV) Is talking about Jesus, by whose stripes you were healed.

Prosperity is in ALL Aspects of Life!

SUPPLY ALL MY NEEDS

PRAYER

We give thanks to God for this day, in which Our dream will flourish, our plans will succeed, Our destiny will be assured, and the desire of our heart will succeed. In Christ Jesus, amen.

The Divine Exchange covers salvation, healing, and financial prosperity. Many people, unfortunately, will accept *salvation* and reject healing and financial prosperity, which God has also provided for us. God wants only the best for us in every area of our lives and has provided a way for us to have it. Step number one, is to understand and accept what God's Will is for us;

<u>GOD'S WILL</u> Putting God first is realizing it's all about Him. Everything in our life is to be directed to Him. Our every breath is to go back to Him. Our every thought is to be for Him.

And do not be conformed to this world, but be transformed by the renewing of your mind, that you may prove what the Will of God is, that which is good and acceptable and perfect. Romans 12:2 (NKJV) "Teach me to do Your will, for You are my God. May Your Gracious Spirit Lead me forward on a Firm Footing" (on Level Ground) Psalm 143:10 (NIV).

We learn more and more about His character and how His perfect Will is working itself out in our own life. Deepening our understanding of God also deepens our faith and desire to worship. God invites us to bring our burdens and needs to Him in prayer.

"Roll your works upon the Lord [commit and trust them wholly to Him; He will cause your thoughts to become agreeable to His will, and] so shall your plans be established and succeed." Proverbs 16:3 (AMPC).

(Cause our thoughts to become agreeable to His will and by being agreeable our prayer gets answered).

When Jesus went to the cross, he provided everything for us that we would ever need. All we need to do is to accept it and to receive it by faith. Many people spend their entire lives waiting for God to do what he has already done. You don't have to wait for God to save you because you know that he is already provided for that. And you know that all you need to do is repent of your sins and to receive Jesus as our Savior to experience the Salvation that God has provided.

The Bible tells us in Romans chapter 10:9-10 that to receive salvation we must confess with our mouth and believe in our heart. That is also the way that we should are supposed to receive healing and prosperity. Confess healing with your mouth and believe in your heart, confess prosperity with your mouth and believe in your heart. It all works the same way.

COVENANT OF WEALTH

but you shall remember the Lord your God: for it is he who gives you power to get wealth, that he may establish his covenant which he swore to your fathers, as it is this day. Deuteronomy 8:18 (ESV).

The word *established,* as used in this verse means to *continue,* when translated into Hebrew. God gives us power, or ability to get wealth because He made a covenant with our fathers and wealth is part of the covenant. Jesus told us>see Luke 13:10-16 (ESV) that healing is also part of the covenant.

The word wealth, as translated in this verse means plenteous in goods. It means in God's Covenant is for us to have plenty of goods. Now don't get crazy on me that doesn't necessarily mean that God wants everyone to be a millionaire but it does mean that God wants us to have nice things. I realize that people have a hard time with this but as we read through the Bible we will discover that God's Word shows that it is his will for us to be prosperous. God never wants us to be poor.

Many preachers are what I call poverty preachers and the people in their churches are poor. God's desire that we have nice things but it is not God's desire that we love these things or covet things. The Bible tells us that the love of money is the root of all evil, it does not tell us that money is the root of all evil. Money is not evil but the love of money is evil. Rich people who love money and poor people who love money and it is evil in both cases. It is not noble to be poor because the Bible even tells us that **poverty is a curse.**

Jesus said I am come that you might have life and have it more abundantly. John 10:10 (NIV). I say that if Jesus came so that we could have an abundant life the least we can do is live an abundant life. Someone has to pay the bills and people who have more than enough money are the people who pay the bills. It takes money for evangelism, to keep the lights on in the church, to send a television signal which carries the gospel into the Moslem countries, to pay the preacher and to feed the poor.

The rule of thumb is from Matthew 6:33 (KJV) when Jesus said, Seek ye first the Kingdom of God and his righteousness and everything you need will be given to you. My dear brothers and sisters this is not poverty. Having everything you need given unto you is prosperity and that is what Jesus said we could have..

POVERTY IS
A CURSE

I t is important that we realize from reading the Bible that
God considers *poverty to be a curse*. We find this to be true
when we look at Job's story. God was blessing him with
health and *abundance*; however, it was when Satan intervened
that God's blessings were interrupted. Let's read it.

"Does Job fear God for nothing?" Satan replied. "Have
you not put a hedge around him and his household and
everything he has? You have blessed the work of his hands,
so that his flocks and herds are spread throughout the land"
Job 1:9-10 (NIV).

When Job was under attack from the devil he encountered
poverty, sickness and calamity. After Job survived the devil's
attack, ***everything was restored*** and he lived a long prosperous
life of enjoying God's blessing.

PRAYER

We thank You oh God for your generosity and kindness, and ask that You hear our whispers of prayer for every need we have. Make us worthy of Your blessing and keep us from further want. We pray in Christ Jesus, amen.

THE LORD IS MY SHEPHERD

The Lord is my Shepherd. Psalm 23:1 (KJV). How many times have we read that verse and how many people really understand it? The key to understanding this verse, is understanding David's relationship with God. David had a very unique relationship with God in as much as God was not only his Salvation, but also his Protector and Provider.

To David, his Salvation with God was the most important thing in the world, to him. We get insight into that relationship in Psalm 51 after David said He had sinned and was asking God for forgiveness and even tried to make a deal with God and said restore to me the Joy of thy Salvation and uphold me with thy free spirit then will I teach transgressors (one who breaks a law or violates a command) thy ways and sinners shall become converted unto thee. David was actually saying to God, if you will forgive me and take me back I will bring people to you. This goes along the lines of what people say the day they got saved. Lord; if you will forgive me and accept me I will serve you all the days of my life.

David not only depended on God to provide for him but he also depended on God for his very breath and so do we all though some people may not appreciate this fact or even believe it. Read more about how David depended upon God. Psalm 62:5-12 (GNT).

In Matthew it goes right along with when Jesus said Seek ye first the kingdom of God and his righteousness and everything you need shall be given unto you. Matthew 6:33 (KJV). Jesus, said everything you need no specifics.

The Lord is my Shepherd I shall not want. To the Sheep, the Shepherd is the most important thing in the world to them. They depend on the Shepherd for guidance, for protection, and for their provision. The sheep hear the Shepherd's voice and another voice they will not follow. The sheep listen for the Shepherd's voice and will never be fooled by an imposter. Are you listening? If the Lord Truly is our Shepherd and we listen for the Shepherd's voice we also shall not want. This is one of the keys to understanding increase in the Kingdom of God.

THE PROSPEROUS SOUL

Beloved, I wish above all things that you may Prosper and be in Health even as your Soul Prospers. III John 2 (NKJV).

Prosperity begins in the Soul.

Here is the secret to becoming prosperous in the kingdom of God. The word soul in this verse, as translated from the Greek means *spirit* and *mind*. In other words we must *prosper* in our *spirit* and in our *mind* before we *prosper* in our bank account. Another way of putting this is that when we *prosper* in our *soul* our bank account will follow.

HOW DO I PROSPER MY SOUL?

The answer to that question is *that you prosper your soul by filling it with God's Word*. The more of God's Word that we hear the more prosper our soul will become.

A PROSPEROUS SOUL IS A KINGDOM MENTALITY

A person with a Kingdom Mentality is a person who understands that God is our Heavenly Father and we are children of the

King and as such are not supposed to be poor or sick. A person with a Kingdom Mentality believes that they are supposed to be prosperous, that they are supposed to have enough money to pay their bills and money left over to help the poor and for every good work .

Note: we can make unwise decisions but, God said we will not be utterly cast down that he will catch us with his right hand. Psalm 37:24 (NIV).

How can I tell if my *Soul is Prospering*?

Our thinking and our attitude *will change*. Jewish people, for the most part have a prosperous soul and that is why as a group they are prosperous people. They believe they are supposed to be prosperous and they are. A person with a prosperous soul will believe that they are supposed to be prosperous.

A Prosperous Soul is an excited Soul

When your soul is prosperous and your level of faith as high we become excited because we are anticipating the blessings of God. A person who is not excited about the things of God is a person who has no faith in God's ability or desire to give them good things. *I know that God is going to provide all of my needs according to his riches in glory by Christ Jesus.*

GUIDE ME LORD

Guide us lord, You are our heart You are our strength, You are our hope. Teach us Lord, and guide our way I love you more each passing day.

It had taken forty years for God to get Egypt out of the hearts of the people before He could bring them into the promised land. Before we are going to go into the promised land we must also get the *wilderness mentality* out of our heart and begin to believe that God loves us and wants only the best for us.

BE FILLED WITH THE FULLNESS OF GOD

Many religions have what they believe are holy sites or buildings, but the God of Love has chosen us to be His dwelling place, if we are willing. The God who created the universe is not impressed with our buildings and shrines. This is what the LORD says: "Heaven is My throne and the earth is My footstool. Where then is a house you could build for Me? Isaiah 66:1 (KJV). And where is a place that I may rest? "For My hand made all these things, Thus all these things came into being," declares the LORD. See Isaiah 66 – (NAS). "But to this one I will look, To him who is humble and contrite of spirit, and who trembles at My word. Isaiah 66:1–2 (NIV). The Lord is looking for a person who is humble before Him and who takes His word very seriously, even to the point of *obedience.* God and His *love* will live inside of this person.

We were created to love. We are made in the image of the God of love. Our purpose is to give love and receive love. God made us in His image so that we could experience His love. God desires to have the most intimate relationship with us as possible. That is, we in God and God in us, united in Love. This is why Jesus came to earth so that He could restore our ultimate purpose of a Holy relationship with God.

Jesus prayed that the same love that God the Father would be in us. "I have made you known to them, and will continue to make you known in order that the love you have for me may be in them and that I myself may be in them." John 17:26 (NIV) When Jesus says, "I have declared unto them thy name", John 17:26 (KJV) it means that He has made God known to the people. It means that He revealed God's character and His power, and He continues to do so.

As Jesus walked the earth His mission was to reveal the heart of His Father, the God of Love. God sent His Son to reveal His love. It is through knowing God, Heart to Heart, that we come to experience His love. Your mission is to experience and reveal the love of God; just as Jesus did. Jesus continues to reveal the Father through His body, the church (us), which includes everyone who is a believer if we are willing.

For this reason I bow my knees to the Father of our Lord Jesus Christ, from whom the whole family in heaven and earth is named, that He would grant you, according to the riches of His glory, to be strengthened with might through His Spirit in the inner man, that Christ may dwell in your hearts through faith; that you, being rooted and grounded in love, may be able to comprehend with all the saints what is the **width** and **length** and **depth** and **height**; to know the love of Christ which passes knowledge; that you may be filled with all the fullness of God. Ephesians 3:14-19 (NIV).

A PRAYER FOR BEING GRATEFUL

Lord God, may we be grateful for our lot, and compassionate toward all those who are suffering every kind of distress at this difficult time. May we hold back nothing, and hasten to be the ministers of whispers of prayer and mercy, like the disciples of Him who went about doing good in times of need such as the church in Jerusalem gave their money freely to help the poor such as Stephen. I think of the verse; We give thanks to God always for you all, making mention of you in our prayers ... I Thess 1:2-3 (KJV).

Thou shalt make the way prosperous, and then thou shalt have good success. I now give a pattern of success and prosperity to the deeper mind within me, which is the law. I now identify myself with the infinite source of supply. I listen to the still, small voice of God within me. This inner voice leads, guides and governs all of my activities. I am one with the abundance of God. I know and believe that there are new and better ways of conducting my business; infinite intelligence reveals the new ways to me.

I am growing in wisdom and understanding. My business is God's business. I am divinely prospered in all ways. Divine wisdom within the reveals the ways and means by which all my affairs are adjusted in the right way immediately.

The words of faith and conviction which I now speak open up all the necessary doors or avenues for my success and prosperity. I know that the Lord or law will perfect that which concerns me. My feet are kept in the perfect pass, because I am a son of the living God.

DOUBLE FOR YOUR TROUBLE

Move Forward

66 "Remember not the former things, nor consider the things of old. Behold, I am doing a new thing; now it springs forth, do you not perceive it? I will make a way in the wilderness and rivers in the desert." Isaiah 43:18–19 (NKJV).

Oftentimes, we get stuck in life because we've been hurt or betrayed, and we end up settling where we are. We allow the disappointment to keep us from the divine appointment. Don't let that be you! Don't let what somebody did or didn't do for you be an excuse to live sour. Don't let a bad break, a divorce, a betrayal or a bad childhood cause you to settle where you are. Move forward and God will pay you back. Move forward and God will vindicate you. May times in our life we come up against a brick wall and we start seeking for help. I have been there many times. We must Move forward and try our best to make the right decision. A new beginning comes forth with gladness and assurance knowing we did our best and it is the best decision.

Nothing that has happened to us is a surprise to God he is with us and holding our hand and allowing circumstances to take place to direct us forward and He plants upon our Heart. The loss of that loved one didn't catch God off guard. I have been in that situation and you wonder why? The business that didn't make it, the relationship that didn't work out (the person that betrayed you) did not stop God's plan for our life. Now, the real question is: are we going to get stuck, fall into self-pity, become bitter and cold, let the past poison our future? Or, are we going to shake it off and move forward knowing that our best days are still up ahead? At times we have a struggle knowing what are we going to do in this situation, we get exhausted and think what must I do. In Isaiah God gives us a double portion of our trouble. Yes, In Isaiah Promises are made to the Jews returned out of captivity, which EXTEND to all those who, through grace, are delivered out of spiritual bondage or slavery. Those who have the Lord for their portion, have reason to say, that they have worthy portion, and to rejoice in it. In the fullness of heaven's joys we shall receive more than double for all our services and sufferings. God desires truth, and therefore hates all injustice.

Instead of your shame you will have a double portion, And instead of humiliation they will shout for joy over their portion. Therefore they will possess a double portion in their land, Everlasting joy will be theirs. We shall enjoy great plenty of all kind of blessings, temporal and spiritual: everlasting joy shall be to us (see Isaiah 35:10). Isaiah 61:7 (NASB).

Every blessing given out is also given to us through the seed of Abraham – If we stand good and someone does us wrong we shall receive DOUBLE PORTION of BLESSING for standing for what is GOOD and RIGHT.

"It's our journey, and ours alone.
Others may walk it with us,
but no one can walk it for us."

God is within her, she will not fall;
God will help her at break of day.
Psalm 46:5 (NIV)

**Amazing Grace how sweet the sound that
saved a *wretch like me...!***
by writer John Newton

We can live our life with *joy, peace,* and *confidence.*

Let go of those disempowering thoughts and reclaim who and Whose we are. We are more than enough. We are the Beloved, in whom God is well pleased.

As you read my notes of my *memoir* and *devotions,* you will be convinced of one all-important truth: you are loved. Like Peter said 'whom shall we go'.

I truly pray that everyone will be as *'blessed'* by reading my *'memoir and devotions'* as I was in writing **Whispers of God to the Hungry Heart.**

ABOUT THE AUTHOR

I am a lady who loves God with all her Heart and I represent God in the highest Honor - Let Happiness Light the Way - There is only one way to happiness and that is to cease worrying about things which are beyond the power of our will - Finding our Destiny is in the Obedience of God and the Joy comes forth in knowing ALL IS WELL between us and the MASTER.

Printed in the United States
By Bookmasters